INTRODUCTION TO FUND ACCOUNTING

INTRODUCTION TO FUND ACCOUNTING

Edward S. Lynn
Joan W. Thompson

University of Arizona
Tucson, Arizona

RESTON PUBLISHING COMPANY, INC., Reston, Virginia 22090

A Prentice-Hall Company

Library of Congress Cataloging in Publication Data

Lynn, Edward S
   Introduction to fund accounting.

   1. Corporations, Nonprofit—Accounting. 2. Account-
ing. I. Thompson, Joan W., 1939-   joint author.
II. Title.
HF5686.N56L85   657'.98   74-13636
ISBN 0-87909-366-8
ISBN 0-87909-365-X (pbk.)

© 1974 by
RESTON PUBLISHING COMPANY, INC.
A Prentice-Hall Company
Box 547
Reston, Virginia 22090

10 9 8 7 6 5 4 3 2 1

Printed in the United States of America.

PREFACE

When the senior author of this text came to the University of Arizona in 1965, the Public Administration Department was requiring an accounting course for its students. Because of the lack of a text that would permit the study of fund accounting in one semester, the subject matter of the course was financial accounting for profit-seeking organizations. They were delighted when he proposed to teach a course in fund accounting to the Public Administration students.

The first effort was based on a combination of a conventional accounting principles book and a conventional fund accounting text. (All fund accounting texts assumed a prior knowledge of accounting for profit-seeking enterprises.) While the first effort was not a failure, neither was it an unqualified success. The senior professor then wrote a short "handout" to give the students an introduction solely to fund accounting. Combined during the first weeks of the semester with simple problems, the handout provided a good introduction to the subject of fund accounting and permitted the students to move into a conventional fund accounting text for most of the semester.

Introduction to Fund Accounting is a major expansion of the handout—but it is designed to serve the same purpose. In its "first edition" it was used in the second semester of 1972-73. With the combination of an *Introduction* and a conventional fund accounting text, we have found that Public Administration and other nonbusiness majors have the tools for a thorough one-semester course.

We want to thank those Public Administration students of the past who have proved feasible a fund accounting course for those who have had no prior accounting.

Many employees of governments and institutions begin work with no accounting background, then find they need to know what is going on in accounting in their offices. We believe that the same qualities that make this book a good introduction to fund accounting in a college course make it suitable for familiarization of municipal, state, and institutional personnel with what accounting in their environment is all about. Its wording is simple, its terminology is well-defined, and its pace is suited to self-study. We expect that those who use it will find their interest stimulated and will want to go on with a more advanced accounting text.

Edward S. Lynn
Joan W. Thompson

CONTENTS

INTRODUCTION TO FUND ACCOUNTING

1

BASIC PRINCIPLES

Accounting is the art of analyzing, recording, summarizing, interpreting, and communicating the results of the economic activities of social and legal entities. Although accounting is frequently referred to as "the language of business," and indeed it serves as a principal means of communication for the profitseeking segment of the economy—it is equally the language of the not-for-profit segment.

Examples of not-for-profit organizations are governments (city, county, state, and federal), universities, hospitals, and a great variety of charitable organizations. They perform many of the services our society considers essential. In fact, they account for approximately one-third of the Gross National Product.

The typical not-for-profit organization is principally financed by taxes or donations. These taxes or donations are usually levied or given for specific purposes, and are to be held or used in accordance with laws, rules, regulations, or contractual requirements. Not-for-profit accounting is frequently referred to as *fund accounting*. The term *fund,* as it is used in not-for-profit accounting, has a specific, technical meaning. The National Committee on Governmental Accounting[1] defines a fund as:

> ... an independent fiscal and accounting entity with a self-balancing set of

---

[1] The Committee was organized in 1934 to develop and help put into effect sound principles and procedures of governmental budgeting, accounting, and reporting.

accounts recording cash and/or other resources together with all related liabilities, obligations, reserves, and equities which are segregated for the purpose of carrying on specific activities or attaining certain objectives in accordance with special regulations, restrictions, or limitations.[2]

The activities of not-for-profit organizations are carried on through one or several different types of funds. Although only the General Fund will be covered in this text, the other funds recommended by the National Committee on Governmental Accounting are: Special Revenue, or Special Funds; Capital Projects Funds; Debt Service Funds; Trust and Agency Funds; Intragovernmental Service Funds; Special Assessment Funds, and Enterprise Funds. For a further discussion of these funds, you may refer to a standard governmental text.

ENTITY CONCEPT

Entity means "one, a unit." All economic activity is carried on by an entity of some sort, be it an individual, a family, a corner grocery, a large corporation, a charitable society, or a governmental unit. The accounting process is applied to entities. For example, if a man owns two businesses, he will have three separate entities—himself (or his family), "Business One," and "Business Two"—each of which is to be accounted for separately.

This text will concern itself primarily with the accounting processes used in one example of not-for-profit organizations—the city. The accounting for cities is very much like the accounting for any other not-for-profit unit or entity—a school district, a state, the nation, a university, or a charitable organization. The city typically renders service without profit and without relationship to the payment made to the city in the form of taxes; its assets, liabilities, revenues, and expenditures pertain to separately established funds that constitute separate accounting entities.

THE ACCOUNTING EQUATION

Property consists of all the goods, real estate, and rights that, taken together, constitute wealth. Each piece of property is owned by a legal entity, and the right of ownership pertains directly to the property. Thus, if the General Fund of a city has cash of $10,000 and taxes receivable from its taxpayers of $2,000, it has property rights applicable to the properties in amounts equal to their values. We can construct an equation for the General Fund as follows:

Cash	+	*Taxes Receivable*	=	*Property Rights*
$10,000	+	$2,000	=	$12,000

For accounting purposes, we speak of property as *assets*, which may be defined as "things of value owned." Property rights are called *equities*. In the foregoing equation the Fund's equity in the assets is $12,000, the amount of the property rights.

---

[2] National Committee on Governmental Accounting, *Governmental Accounting, Auditing, and Financial Reporting.* 1968. pp. 6-7.

	Assets		=	Equities

		Assets		=	Equities
Cash	+	Taxes Receivable		=	Equities
$10,000	+	$2,000		=	$12,000

But suppose that the city has had to borrow money—that there are notes payable to banks of $1,500. The banks (creditors) have an equity in the assets; if the agreed payments are not made, the banks may use the courts to force the city to make payment. The equation to include the notes payable is as follows:

		Assets		=	Equities		
		Taxes			Creditors'		Residual
Cash	+	Receivable		=	Equity	+	Equity
$10,000	+	$2,000		=	$1,500	+	$10,500

The creditors' equity is ordinarily referred to as a *liability*; liabilities are defined as "amounts owed." The term *residual equity* is descriptive of the nature of the city's equity because the creditors have first claim on the assets and the city would have the assets left after the creditors' claims are satisfied. The residual equity, when describing not-for-profit organizations, may be referred to as *fund balance*.

Assets	=	Equities		
Assets	=	Liabilities	+	Fund Balance

Assets are always equal to equities. As indicated above, equities are of two basic kinds: those of the creditors and that of the entity (i.e., the fund being accounted for). The equity of the entity may be computed by taking the basic equation:

Assets	=	Liabilities	+	Fund Balance

and moving the liabilities to the left side.

Assets	−	Liabilities	=	Fund Balance

This algebraic manipulation of the liabilities illustrates an important point: The accounting equation *is* algebraic, and all rules of algebra apply to changes that are made in the accounting equation of an entity.

2

ANALYSIS OF
TRANSACTIONS

THE ACCOUNT

Records for individual assets, liabilities, and fund balance are kept in accounts. Accounts may take many forms, but the simplest is called a *T-account*. The reason for this name is obvious when we look at one:

Every account has three major parts:

Name

Left or *Debit* Side	Right or *Credit* Side

The name of the asset, liability, or fund balance that the account is kept for is placed on the horizontal line.

The use of accounts originated as early as Roman times, and the same Latin words that gave rise to our terms *debtor* and *creditor* gave rise to terms that are used in connection with accounts. The term *debit* is used as an adjective, meaning "left"; as a verb, "to place on the left side of the account"; or as a noun, "the amount that is placed on the left side of the account." Similarly, *credit* means "right," "to place on the right side of the account," or "the amount that is placed on the right side of the account." *The terms, in and of themselves, do not carry any increase-decrease meaning.*

A uniform assignment of increase-decrease meanings to the left and right sides of the accounts has been accepted in the United States. These meanings are assigned on the basis of the type of account: asset, liability, or fund balance.

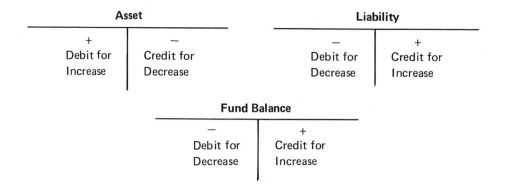

This same relationship is illustrated below:

Type of Account	Normal Balance	To Increase	To Decrease
Asset	Debit	Debit	Credit
Liability	Credit	Credit	Debit
Fund Balance	Credit	Credit	Debit

TRANSACTION ANALYSIS

A *transaction* is an economic event that affects the assets or equities of a fund. The effects of the event must be recorded as changes in the accounting equation; that is, they must be recorded in the proper accounts. The recording of every transaction will be composed of an equal dollar amount of debits and credits. To illustrate the effects of transactions on assets and equities, as well as the debit-credit relationship, the following transactions of a General Fund will be analyzed.

TRANSACTION 1.   The City Council levied property taxes of $50,000.00.

Analysis

Accounts Affected	Type of Account	Change in Balance	Debit	Credit
Taxes Receivable	Asset	Increase	$50,000	
Fund Balance	Fund Balance	Increase		$50,000

Effect on accounts

Taxes Receivable		Fund Balance	
50,000			50,000

Transaction 1 states that the City's taxing power was used to create an asset, taxes receivable from taxpayers, for the General Fund to use. Since at the time of the levy the asset, taxes receivable, was created, the balance of the General Fund was therefore created as the offsetting (balancing) property right.

To determine the amount of the tax levy several steps were needed. The tax assessor had to identify all of the property in the City and place a value upon all that was not exempt from taxation by virtue of types of owners (e.g., churches, city, county, or state). The City Council took note of the amount of money needed from property taxes and levied a tax of a specified amount per dollar of property valuation.

Note that at the time of the levy *no cash changed hands*. The City received a new asset as a result of the levy; the acquisition of an asset increased the residual equity.

TRANSACTION 2. The City Council borrowed $10,000.00 from the local bank by means of tax anticipation notes.

Analysis

Accounts Affected	Type of Account	Change in Balance	Debit	Credit
Cash	Asset	Increase	$10,000	
Notes Payable	Liability	Increase		$10,000

Effect on accounts

Cash		Notes Payable	
10,000			10,000

The taxes levied in Transaction 1 may not have been due until several months after the levy, and they were not likely to be collected in full even when due. In Transaction 2 the City borrowed money with which to operate until collections occurred; in order to get the cash, it promised to pay back the loan at a future date. Thus, it added to its assets and created a liability without affecting the City's residual equity.

TRANSACTION 3.   Citizens paid to the General Fund $45,000.00 of the taxes levied in Transaction 1.

Analysis

Accounts Affected	Type of Account	Change in Balance	Debit	Credit
Cash	Asset	Increase	$45,000	
Taxes Receivable	Asset	Decrease		$45,000

Effect on accounts

Cash	Taxes Receivable
45,000	45,000

In Transaction 3 the City received cash, an asset, but at the same time surrendered claims to an asset, taxes receivable, of an equal amount. Hence, there was no change in total assets. Because the taxes had previously been set up as an asset and at that time had caused an increase of $50,000.00 in the balance of the fund, *no increase in the fund balance occurred at the time of the collection of the taxes receivable.*

TRANSACTION 4.   The City paid its employees $25,000.00. This transaction has two elements: (1) The recognition that the City owes its employees for work performed[1]; (2) The actual payment. Each of these two elements must be recognized in analyzing the transaction and in recording it in the accounts.

Analysis, recognition of liability

Accounts Affected	Type of Account	Change in Balance	Debit	Credit
Fund Balance	Fund Balance	Decrease	$25,000	
Vouchers Payable	Liability	Increase		$25,000

---

[1] Governments and businesses have found that it is necessary to require a routine for approval of a payment if control over disbursements is to be maintained. Hence, in this text we shall assume that all disbursements require the authority of a voucher, which is the physical evidence that all of the checks have been applied to a proposed disbursement and that the City has a valid debt payable to the creditor listed in the voucher.

Effect on accounts

Fund Balance		Vouchers Payable	
25,000			25,000

Analysis, payment of liability

Accounts Affected	Type of Account	Change in Balance	Debit	Credit
Vouchers Payable	Liability	Decrease	$25,000	
Cash	Asset	Decrease		$25,000

Effect on accounts

Vouchers Payable		Cash	
25,000			25,000

In the first entry a liability is created because the City owes its employees for providing to the public the services expected of the City. Fund balance is decreased by the recognition of the debt—*note that there is neither a corresponding increase in an asset account nor a corresponding decrease in another liability account.* The second entry records the paying of the voucher, which results in a decrease in the liability account (because the City no longer owes the amount of the voucher) and a decrease in the asset, cash.

TRANSACTION 5. The City bought materials and supplies for which it paid its suppliers $21,000.00. Like Transaction 4, this transaction has two elements.

Analysis, recognition of liability

Accounts Affected	Type of Account	Change in Balance	Debit	Credit
Fund Balance	Fund Balance	Decrease	$21,000	
Vouchers Payable	Liability	Increase		$21,000

Effect on accounts

Fund Balance		Vouchers Payable	
21,000			21,000

Analysis, payment of liability

Accounts Affected	Type of Account	Change in Balance	Debit	Credit
Vouchers Payable	Liability	Decrease	$21,000	
Cash	Asset	Decrease		$21,000

Effect on accounts

Vouchers Payable		Cash	
21,000			21,000

The rationale for these entries is the same as that of Transaction 4. In the first entry a liability is created because the City owes a creditor for the materials and supplies that have been used to provide to the public the services expected of the City. Fund balance is decreased by the recognition of the liability—*there is neither a corresponding increase in an asset account[2] nor a corresponding decrease in another liability account.* The second entry records the paying of the voucher, which results in a decrease in the liability and a decrease in the asset, cash.

TRANSACTION 6.   The City paid tax anticipation notes of $7,500.00. This transaction has two elements.

Analysis, transfer of liability

Accounts Affected	Type of Account	Change in Balance	Debit	Credit
Notes Payable	Liability	Decrease	$7,500	
Vouchers Payable	Liability	Increase		$7,500

Effect on accounts

Notes Payable		Vouchers Payable	
7,500			7,500

---

[2] As a matter of fact, the materials and supplies bought during a fiscal period *are* on hand (and are assets) for varying lengths of time. However, most cities do not attempt to record them as assets; for accounting purposes, they are treated as if they were consumed immediately. In many jurisdictions, the law requires this treatment; in others, the treatment described is a matter of custom.

Analysis, payment of liability

Accounts Affected	Type of Account	Change in Balance	Debit	Credit
Vouchers Payable	Liability	Decrease	$7,500	
Cash	Asset	Decrease		$7,500

Effect on accounts

Vouchers Payable		Cash	
7,500			7,500

In Transaction 6 the City repaid a portion of its notes to the bank. This transaction is similar to Transactions 4 and 5—a liability must be paid. The difference here, in the first entry of Transaction 6, is that there is no decrease in fund balance because the increase in one liability is offset by the decrease in another liability. The second entry records the paying of the voucher, with a resultant decrease in the liability (the City no longer owes it) and a decrease in the asset, cash.

THE LEDGER

All the accounts that have been used in the illustrations thus far comprise the General Ledger of the General Fund. A *ledger* is a group of accounts. The reasons the accounts belong in a group may vary considerably; other ledgers will be presented as necessary. The financial transactions of the General Fund will always be recorded, either in complete detail or in summary fashion, in the General Ledger of the General Fund.

If all of the entries that have been given so far were recorded in the T-accounts of the General Ledger of the General Fund, the accounts would look like this (the numbers in parenthesis refer to the transaction number):

Cash				Taxes Receivable			
(2)	10,000	25,000	(4)	(1)	50,000	45,000	(3)
(3)	45,000	21,000	(5)				
	55,000	7,500	(6)		5,000		
1,500		53,500					

Notes Payable				Vouchers Payable			
(6)	7,500	10,000	(2)	(4)	25,000	25,000	(4)
		2,500		(5)	21,000	21,000	(5)
				(6)	7,500	7,500	(6)
					53,500	53,500	

Fund Balance

(4)	25,000	50,000	(1)	
(5)	21,000	*4,000*		
	46,000			

THE TRIAL BALANCE

The *trial balance* is a list of all of the accounts in a ledger and of their balances. The purpose of the trial balance is to prove the equality of the debits and credits in the ledger. Maintaining the equality of debits and credits automatically maintains the equality of the accounting equation as changes occur in its components.

To prepare a trial balance, the following steps should be followed:

1. "Pencil foot" all accounts having two or more debits or two or more credits. This means that small pencil figures will indicate the total debits and the total credits of each account (where there are two or more figures on either side). See the preceding accounts for illustrations.

2. Determine account balances by calculating the difference between the debit and credit totals in each account. The difference is termed the *balance* of the account; it is described as a debit or credit balance, depending on which side of the account is larger, and is penciled in on the side that is larger. For example, in the preceding illustration Cash has a debit balance of $1,500.

3. List each account and its balance on paper that has two dollar columns. Debit balances will be placed in the left column and credit balances in the right. If the ledger is in balance, total debits will equal total credits. The illustration that follows is a trial balance of the General Ledger after the foregoing entries have been placed in the accounts.

CITY OF BALLARD
GENERAL FUND
TRIAL BALANCE
December 31, 19X5

Cash	1,500	
Taxes Receivable	5,000	
Notes Payable		2,500
Fund Balance		4,000
	6,500	6,500

The heading of the trial balance should completely identify it as the trial balance of a specific city and ledger at a specific date. Many types of schedules are prepared in a typical city, and the passage of time dulls memories as to what an unidentified set of figures means. A typical city has a number of funds, and a trial balance of each is usually taken at least monthly. The need for identification is evident.

The trial balance proves the mechanical equality of the account balances, but it does not prove that the accounting is correct. If a figure has been placed on the proper side but in the wrong account, if an incorrect amount has been used for recording a transaction, or if offsetting errors have been made, the trial balance will still be in balance.

Problem 2-1

City of Adamsville

The following transactions summarize the operations of the City of Adamsville for the year ended December 31, 19X5.

1. The City Council levied property taxes of $90,000.
2. The City Council borrowed $20,000 from the local bank by means of tax anticipation notes.
3. Citizens paid to the General Fund $82,000 of the taxes levied in Transactions 1.
4. The City paid its employees $40,000.
5. The City bought materials and supplies for which it paid its suppliers $25,000.
6. The City paid tax anticipation notes of $15,000.

Requirements

1. **Enter transactions in T-accounts.**
2. **Prepare a trial balance.**

Problem 2-2

City of Bartlett

The following transactions summarize the operations of the City of Bartlett for the year ended December 31, 19X5:

1. The City levied property taxes of $250,000.
2. The City borrowed $50,000 from the local bank by means of tax anticipation notes.
3. The City received materials and supplies for which it was billed $25,000.
4. The City received $200,000 for the payment of property taxes.
5. The City paid its employees $65,000.
6. The City paid for the materials and supplies received in Transactions 3.
7. The City discovered it had made an underassessment of property taxes in the amount of $10,000 and levied the additional amount.

8. The City paid tax anticipation notes of $50,000.

Requirements

1. **Enter transactions in T-accounts.**
2. **Prepare a trial balance.**

3

JOURNALIZING AND POSTING

THE GENERAL JOURNAL

The first evidence of a transaction is usually a *business paper*. The paper may, for example, be the cash register tape, the handwritten sales slip, the invoice that accompanies a shipment, or the receipt for rental of a building. These business papers are also referred to as *source documents* because they are the source, or the first evidence, of a transaction. The proper sequence for data to flow from the transaction to the ledger accounts is as follows:

Transaction occurs

↓

Source document is prepared or received

↓

Entry is journalized

↓

Journal entry is posted to the ledger

The desirability of having a chronological and complete record of transactions led to the development of the journal. It, or variations of it, is always prepared and is the basis for postings to the accounts. The group of accounts to which these postings from the journal are made is referred to as a *ledger*. *Posting* is defined as the process of transferring data from the journal to the ledger accounts.

No entry is made in the accounts without the authorization and direction provided by the journal. In its simplest form the journal is called a *General Journal*, which is illustrated below. The transactions journalized are the same ones previously analyzed in Chapter 2.

CITY OF BALLARD
GENERAL FUND
GENERAL JOURNAL

Date	Account Titles	Post Ref.	Debit	Credit
Tr. 1	Taxes Receivable		50,000	
	Fund Balance			50,000
	To record levy of property taxes.			
Tr. 2	Cash		10,000	
	Notes Payable			10,000
	To record loan from bank on tax anticipation notes.			
Tr. 3	Cash		45,000	
	Taxes Receivable			45,000
	To record receipt of taxes levied.			
Tr. 4	Fund Balance		25,000	
	Vouchers Payable			25,000
	To record preparation of voucher for payment of salaries.			
	Vouchers Payable		25,000	
	Cash			25,000
	To record payment of voucher.			
Tr. 5	Fund Balance		21,000	
	Vouchers Payable			21,000
	To record preparation of voucher for materials and supplies.			
	Vouchers Payable		21,000	
	Cash			21,000
	To record payment of voucher.			

Date	Account Titles	Post Ref.	Debit	Credit
Tr. 6	Notes Payable		7,500	
	Vouchers Payable			7,500
	To record preparation of			
	voucher for notes payable.			
	Vouchers Payable		7,500	
	Cash			7,500
	To record payment of voucher.			

Several conventional practices illustrated in the journal should be noted.

1. A column for the date is provided where the year, month, and day will be entered. In the illustration, transaction numbers were used instead of dates because the dates were not given in the problem.
2. The debit part (all of the debits) of the entry is always recorded first and is not indented.
3. The credit part of the entry is indented.
4. Each entry is supported with a brief explanation of the transaction.
5. No dollar signs are used in the journal.
6. A blank line is left between journal entries.

POSTING

Posting has been defined above as the process of transferring data from the journal to the ledger accounts. This transferring of data should be done in the following manner (it should be noted that each ledger account has now been assigned an account number and that the pages in the journal have been numbered):

1. Record in the proper ledger account the date and the amount for each account cited in the journal entry. The journal indicates whether the account should be debited or credited. (When dates are not given in textbook problems, use transaction numbers.)
2. Record the page number of the journal in the posting reference column of the account.
3. Record the account number of the ledger account in the posting reference column of the journal.

It should be noted that the last step in the posting process is to place the account number from the ledger in the posting reference column of the journal. Two purposes are thus served: (1) The account number in the journal and the journal page number in the ledger serve as a cross-reference in the event that it is necessary to trace a figure from one source to another; (2) Placing the general ledger account number in the posting reference column of the journal indicates that the posting of that item is completed. In the event of interruptions during posting, it is then possible to see exactly where posting is to be resumed.

Transaction 1 from the preceding illustration is used below to depict how the general journal and the accounts in the general ledger would appear before and after posting has been completed.

Before posting

CITY OF BALLARD
GENERAL FUND
GENERAL JOURNAL

Page 1

Date	Account Titles	Post Ref.	Debit	Credit
Tr. 1	Taxes Receivable Fund Balance To record levy of property taxes.		50,000	50,000

Taxes Receivable Acct. No. 2   Fund Balance   Acct. No. 5

After posting

CITY OF BALLARD
GENERAL FUND
GENERAL JOURNAL

Page 1

Date	Account Titles	Post Ref.	Debit	Credit
Tr. 1	Taxes Receivable Fund Balance To record levy of property taxes.	2 5	50,000	50,000

Taxes Receivable   Acct. No. 2   Fund Balance   Acct. No. 5

Date	P.R.	Amount		Date	P.R.	Amount
T1	1	50,000		TI	1	50,000

SUMMARY EXAMPLE FOR CITY OF BALLARD

The following example is a summary of the transactions and accounting procedures presented up to this point. The transactions previously presented for the City of Ballard are shown below as they would appear after being journalized and posted. Account balances are ascertained and a trial balance is prepared.

CITY OF BALLARD
GENERAL FUND
GENERAL JOURNAL

Date	Account Titles	Post Ref.	Debit	Credit
Tr. 1	Taxes Receivable	2	50,000	
	Fund Balance	5		50,000
	To record levy of property taxes.			
Tr. 2	Cash	1	10,000	
	Notes Payable	3		10,000
	To record loan from bank on tax anticipation notes.			
Tr. 3	Cash	1	45,000	
	Taxes Receivable	2		45,000
	To record receipt of taxes levied.			
Tr. 4	Fund Balance	5	25,000	
	Vouchers Payable	4		25,000
	To record preparation of voucher for payment of salaries.			
	Vouchers Payable	4	25,000	
	Cash	1		25,000
	To record payment of voucher.			
Tr. 5	Fund Balance	5	21,000	
	Vouchers Payable	4		21,000
	To record preparation of voucher for materials and supplies.			
	Vouchers Payable	4	21,000	
	Cash	1		21,000
	To record payment of voucher.			

Date	Account Titles	Post Ref.	Debit	Credit
Tr. 6	Notes Payable	3	7,500	
	Vouchers Payable	4		7,500
	To record preparation of voucher for notes payable.			
	Vouchers Payable	4	7,500	
	Cash	1		7,500
	To record payment of voucher.			

CITY OF BALLARD
GENERAL FUND
GENERAL LEDGER

Cash   Acct. No. 1

Date	P.R.	Amount	Date	P.R.	Amount
Tr. 2	J1	10,000	Tr. 4	J1	25,000
Tr. 3	J1	45,000	Tr. 5	J1	21,000
	1,500	*55,000*	Tr. 6	J2	7,500
					53,000

Taxes Receivable   Acct. No. 2

Date	P.R.	Amount	Date	P.R.	Amount
Tr. 1	J1	50,000	Tr. 3	J1	45,000
	5,000				

Notes Payable   Acct. No. 3

Date	P.R.	Amount	Date	P.R.	Amount
Tr. 6	J2	7,500	Tr. 2	J1	10,000
				2,500	

Vouchers Payable   Acct. No. 4

Date	P.R.	Amount	Date	P.R.	Amount
Tr. 4	J1	25,000	Tr. 4	J1	25,000
Tr. 5	J1	21,000	Tr. 5	J1	21,000
Tr. 6	J2	7,500	Tr. 6	J2	7,500
		53,500			*53,500*

Fund Balance   Acct. No. 5

Date	P.R.	Amount	Date	P.R.	Amount
Tr. 4	J1	25,000	Tr. 1	J1	50,000
Tr. 5	J1	21,000		*4,000*	
		46,000			

CITY OF BALLARD
GENERAL FUND
TRIAL BALANCE
December 31, 19X5

Cash	1,500	
Taxes Receivable	5,000	
Notes Payable		2,500
Fund Balance		4,000
	6,500	6,500

Problem 3-1

Use the transaction information given in Problem 2-1.

Requirements

1. Journalize the transactions in a General Journal.
2. Post the General Journal entries to the accounts in the General Ledger.
3. Ascertain account balances.
4. Prepare a trial balance.

Problem 3-2

Use the transaction information given in Problem 2-2.

Requirements

1. Journalize the transactions in a General Journal.
2. Post the General Journal entries to the accounts in the General Ledger.
3. Ascertain account balances.
4. Prepare a trial balance.

4

TEMPORARY FUND BALANCE ACCOUNTS

As the size of a city or other organization increases, the complexity of its operations makes it desirable to record transactions that affect fund balance in accounts that facilitate analysis of the changes in fund balance. If only the Fund Balance account itself were used to record increases in fund balance, there would be many kinds of increases in the one account. There are revenues coming in from many different sources such as property taxes, licenses, and parking meter receipts. In these circumstances it would be much better to have separate accounts in which to record the increases in fund balance. During the year individual accounts for all the different kinds of revenues are maintained so that at the end of the year the accountant can say to the city manager, "Property taxes produced X dollars, parking meters produced Y dollars, and licenses and permits produced Z dollars."

With detailed information about revenues the city manager will be able to plan for the future and more capably control the present. He can look back at what has happened in the past and say, "We got this much in the past. We should get more (or less) in the future because of these changes in circumstances." Perhaps equally important, he can compare this year's actual revenues from these various sources with his estimates. Where differences are significant, he should try to figure out what went wrong either with the estimates or with actual performance. Having identified the problem, he can move to correct it.

REVENUES AND EXPENDITURES

A charitable organization, for example, may receive assets that increase fund balance (the increases in fund balance during a designated period of time are called *revenue*) from a number of sources: individual donations; the United Fund; local, state, or federal grants; or payments for services if those benefited are able to pay in whole or in part. Similarly, a charitable organization may spend its resources for many purposes; control of expenditures can only be maintained if the top management can authorize individuals to spend the resources and can know who spent them and for what purposes. Hence, the expenditures are usually recorded in individual accounts indicating the purpose of the expenditure and hence, indirectly, the person responsible for it.

Thus, we may expand the equation by the addition of revenues and expenditures:

$$Assets \ = \ Liabilities \ + \ Fund \ Balance \ + \ Revenues \ - \ Expenditures$$

Revenues and Expenditures are temporary accounts; they are parts of fund balance, and at any point in time the correct *total* balance of the fund can only be identified by adding Revenues to the Fund Balance account and deducting Expenditures from the sum. The calculation of total fund balance *in the accounts* is typically performed only once per year; at other times informal calculation usually suffices.

The Revenues and Expenditures accounts derive their increase-decrease sides from their relationship to Fund Balance. In the equation given above, a plus sign precedes Revenues, as is true of Fund Balance. The accounts are of the same nature; hence, their increase-decrease sides are the same. But the minus sign that precedes Expenditures is the opposite of the plus sign that precedes Fund Balance, and the increase-decrease sides are reversed for Expenditures. To summarize in T-account form, the expanded accounting equation for the General Fund may be shown as follows:

Assets	=	Liabilities	+	Fund Balance	+	Revenues	−	Expenditures
+ | −		− | +		− | +		− | +		+ | −

Now, suppose that the condensed trial balance for a city is as follows:

	Debit	Credit
Assets	20,000	
Liabilities		12,000
Fund Balance		9,000
Revenues		45,000
Expenditures	46,000	
	66,000	66,000

If we express the trial balance in full equation form, it becomes:

$$20,000 \ = \ 12,000 \ + \ 9,000 \ + \ 45,000 \ - \ (+46,000)$$

$$20,000 \ = \ 12,000 \ + \ 9,000 \ + \ 45,000 \ - \ 46,000$$

$$20,000 \ = \ 20,000$$

The debit balance in Expenditures is a plus balance, but because the controlling sign for the account is a minus (that is, because Expenditures are to be deducted from Fund Balance), the effect of the Expenditures account on the right side of the equation is negative.

The following schematic is an expansion of an earlier illustration:

Type of Account	Normal Balance	To Increase	To Decrease
Asset	Debit	Debit	Credit
Liability	Credit	Credit	Debit
Fund Balance:			
Fund Balance	Credit	Credit	Debit
Revenues	Credit	Credit	Debit
Expenditures	Debit	Debit	Credit

Revenues increase Fund Balance; and just as increases in Fund Balance are recorded as credits, increases in Revenues accounts during an accounting period are recorded as credits. Expenditures decrease Fund Balance; and just as decreases in Fund Balance are recorded as debits, increases in Expenditures accounts are recorded as debits.

SUMMARY EXAMPLE FOR CITY OF BALLARD

The following illustration takes the same six transactions previously analyzed for City of Ballard and journalizes them as they would have been journalized if temporary Fund Balance accounts had been in use:

CITY OF BALLARD
GENERAL FUND
GENERAL JOURNAL

Date	Account Titles	Post Ref.	Debit	Credit
Tr. 1	Taxes Receivable		50,000	
	Revenues			50,000
	To record levy of property taxes.			
Tr. 2	Cash		10,000	
	Notes Payable			10,000
	To record loan from bank on tax anticipation notes.			
Tr. 3	Cash		45,000	
	Taxes Receivable			45,000
	To record receipt of taxes levied.			
Tr. 4	Expenditures		25,000	
	Vouchers Payable			25,000
	To record preparation of voucher for payment of salaries.			
	Vouchers Payable		25,000	
	Cash			25,000
	To record payment of voucher.			
Tr. 5	Expenditures		21,000	
	Vouchers Payable			21,000
	To record preparation of voucher for materials and supplies.			
	Vouchers Payable		21,000	
	Cash			21,000
	To record payment of voucher.			

Date	Account Titles	Post Ref.	Debit	Credit
Tr. 6	Notes Payable		7,500	
	Vouchers Payable			7,500
	To record preparation of voucher for notes payable.			
	Vouchers Payable		7,500	
	Cash			7,500
	To record payment of voucher.			

SUMMARY EXAMPLE FOR CITY OF DOWDLE

The following example reviews the principles of fund accounting discussed up to this point. Several transactions may be somewhat unfamiliar, but many are similar to those analyzed for the City of Ballard. It should be noted that some of the accounts in the General Ledger of the City of Dowdle have beginning balances that must be entered directly in the General Ledger accounts before journalizing is begun.

The following steps will be illustrated:

1. Entering beginning balances in the General Ledger.
2. Journalizing the transactions in a General Journal.
3. Posting the General Journal entries to the accounts in the General Ledger.
4. Ascertaining account balances.
5. Preparing a trial balance.

The ledger is generally arranged with Asset, Liability, Fund Balance, Revenue, and Expenditure accounts in that order. Several different numbering systems for the accounts might be used; in this example and others in this text, the accounts are simply numbered consecutively.

CITY OF DOWDLE
GENERAL FUND

The account balances for the General Fund of the City of Dowdle as of January 1, 19X5, were as follows:

Cash	$10,000
Taxes Receivable	3,000
Vouchers Payable	1,000
Fund Balance	12,000

The transactions for the City of Dowdle for 19X5 were as follows:

1. The City levied property taxes in the amount of $200,000.
2. The City borrowed $50,000 on tax anticipation notes. This loan was to be repaid as soon as citizens paid their property taxes.
3. The City purchased materials and supplies on account for $100,000.
4. Citizens paid $100,000 of their property taxes. Prepare a voucher. Also refer to Transaction 2 for additional entry.
5. The City paid the entire balance of vouchers payable.
6. Cash was received from the following sources:

Parking meter collections	$30,000	Cr. Revenues
Refund on overcharge on		
materials	500	Cr. Expenditures
	$30,500	

7. Citizens paid $88,000 of their property taxes.
8. The City paid its employees $105,000.
9. A refund of $1,000 was paid to a citizen on the overassessment and payment of his taxes.

CITY OF DOWDLE
GENERAL FUND
GENERAL JOURNAL

Page 1

Date	Account Titles	Post Ref.	Debit	Credit
Tr. 1	Taxes Receivable	2	200,000	
	Revenues	6		200,000
	To record levy of property taxes.			
Tr. 2	Cash	1	50,000	
	Notes Payable	4		50,000
	To record bank loan on tax anticipation notes			
Tr. 3	Expenditures	7	100,000	
	Vouchers Payable	3		100,000
	To record preparation of voucher of materials and supplies.			
Tr. 4	Cash	1	100,000	
	Taxes Receivable	2		100,000
	To record receipt of taxes previously accrued.			
	Notes Payable	4	50,000	
	Vouchers Payable	3		50,000
	To record preparation of voucher for notes payable.			
	Vouchers Payable	3	50,000	
	Cash	1		50,000
	To record payment of voucher.			
Tr. 5	Vouchers Payable	3	101,000	
	Cash	1		101,000
	To record payment of voucher.			
Tr. 6	Cash	1	30,500	
	Revenues	6		30,000
	Expenditures	7		500
	To record receipt of cash, including refund on materials and supplies.			

Date	Account Titles	Post Ref.	Debit	Credit
Tr. 7	Cash	1	88,000	
	Taxes Receivable	2		88,000
	To record receipt of taxes previously accrued.			
Tr. 8	Expenditures	7	105,000	
	Vouchers Payable	3		105,000
	To record preparation of voucher for salaries.			
	Vouchers Payable	3	105,000	
	Cash	1		105,000
	To record payment of voucher.			
Tr. 9	Revenues	6	1,000	
	Vouchers Payable	3		1,000
	To record refund on over-assessment of taxes.			
	Vouchers Payable	3	1,000	
	Cash	1		1,000
	To record payment of voucher.			

CITY OF DOWDLE
GENERAL FUND
GENERAL LEDGER

Cash   Acct. No. 1

19X5							
Jan.	1 Balance	✓	10,000	Tr.	4	1	50,000
Tr.	2	1	50,000	Tr.	5	1	101,000
Tr.	4	1	100,000	Tr.	8	2	105,000
Tr.	6	1	30,500				
Tr.	7	2	88,000	Tr.	9	2	1,000
		21,500	278,500				257,000

Taxes Receivable   Acct. No. 2

19X5							
Jan.	1 Balance	✓	3,000	Tr.	4	1	100,000
Tr.	1	1	200,000	Tr.	7	2	88,000
		15,000	203,000				188,000

Vouchers Payable   Acct. No. 3

				19X5				
Tr.	4	1	50,000	Jan.	1 Balance	✓		1,000
Tr.	5	1	101,000	Tr.	3		1	100,000
Tr.	8	2	105,000	Tr.	4		1	50,000
Tr.	9	2	1,000	Tr.	8		2	105,000
			257,000	Tr.	9		2	1,000
								257,000

Notes Payable   Acct. No. 4

Tr.	4	1	50,000	Tr.	2	1	50,000

Fund Balance   Acct. No. 5

			19X5		
		Jan.	1 Balance	✓	12,000

Revenues   Acct. No. 6

Tr.	9	2	1,000	Tr.	1	1	200,000
				Tr.	6	1	30,000
			229,000				*230,000*

Expenditures   Acct. No. 7

Tr.	3	1	100,000	Tr.	6	1	500
Tr.	8	2	105,000				
		204,500	*205,000*				

CITY OF DOWDLE
GENERAL FUND
TRIAL BALANCE
December 31, 19X5

Cash	21,500	
Taxes Receivable	15,000	
Fund Balance		12,000
Revenues		229,000
Expenditures	204,500	
	241,000	241,000

Problem 4-1

CITY OF CARTER
GENERAL FUND

The operations of the General Fund of the City of Carter for the calendar year 19X5 are summarized below:

1. The following balances were in the accounts at the beginning of the year:

Cash	$15,000
Fund Balance	15,000

2. The City levied property taxes of $145,000.
3. The City borrowed $30,000 in anticipation of collecting taxes.
4. The City purchased materials and supplies on credit for $40,000.
5. The City received $80,000 from the payment of property taxes.
6. The City discovered it had made an underassessment of property taxes in the amount of $5,000 and levied the additional amount.
7. The City made payment of $25,000 on the materials and supplies purchased in Transaction 4 above.
8. The City made salary payments of $110,000 to employees.
9. The City paid $20,000 on its tax anticipation note liability.
10. The City collected the following:

Property Taxes	$65,000
Miscellaneous Revenues	10,000

11. The City paid the following:

Vouchers Payable	$14,000
Tax Anticipation Notes	10,000

12. The City refunded $1,000 for overassessment that had been paid by a taxpayer.

Requirements

1. **Make General Journal entries.**
2. **Post to accounts in the General Ledger.**
3. **Prepare a trial balance.**

Problem 4-2

CITY OF DANVILLE
LIBRARY FUND

The Library Fund of the City of Danville had beginning balances, January 1, 19X1, of

Cash	$5,000
Fund Balance	5,000

1. Property taxes of $100,000 were levied.
2. The City borrowed $20,000 from a local bank by means of tax anticipation notes until receipts would come in from revenues.
3. The City bought a special vehicle on account for use as a Library Bookmobile—$5,000.
4. The City bought materials and supplies on account for $4,000.
5. Books were bought on account for the Library Bookmobile for $10,000.
6. Cash receipts came in during the year from

Property Taxes	$ 69,500
Miscellaneous Revenues	35,500
	$105,000

7. The City paid off the notes borrowed from the bank in Transaction 2.
8. The City paid payrolls during year of $78,000.
9. The City paid for the vehicle in Transaction 3 and for books in Transaction 5, both of which were purchased on account.
10. Expenses incurred and paid in connection with the operation and maintenance of Bookmobile were $500.

Requirements

1. **Prepare journal entries for the transactions given.**
2. **Post to accounts in the General Ledger.**
3. **Prepare a trial balance from balances in T-accounts.**

5

CLOSING ENTRIES

Revenue and expenditure accounts have been referred to as "temporary" accounts because their balances are transferred into the Fund Balance account at the end of the period. This transferring process is called *closing*. The result is that at the end of the year there is in the Fund Balance account exactly what would have been there if we had recorded increases and decreases in fund balance directly in the Fund Balance account all year, rather than recording them in temporary accounts.

PREPARING CLOSING ENTRIES

To prepare the closing entries, the following steps should be taken:

1. Obtain the balances of the temporary fund balance accounts from the trial balance (which we may now refer to as the *preclosing trial balance*). The preclosing trial balance is the most convenient source of the balances of each of the accounts, though those balances are also available in the accounts themselves.

2. The first closing entry closes the revenue accounts by debiting each revenue account with the amount of its balance and crediting Fund Balance. The revenue accounts will now be *closed* in the sense that the sums of the debits and credits now in the accounts are the same; they have zero balances.

3. The second closing entry closes the expenditure accounts by crediting each expenditure

account with the amount of its balance and debiting Fund Balance. The expenditure accounts will now be *closed* because the sums of the debits and credits now in the accounts are the same; they have zero balances.

POSTCLOSING TRIAL BALANCE

A *postclosing trial balance* can now be prepared; it will contain no balances for the temporary accounts that have now been transferred to Fund Balance. (The prefix *post* means "after"; this trial balance is prepared after closing entries have been journalized and posted.)

Closing entries and a postclosing trial balance for the City of Dowdle (illustrated in Chaper 4) are given below:

CITY OF DOWDLE
GENERAL FUND
GENERAL JOURNAL

Date	Account Titles	Post Ref.	Debit	Credit
Cl. Ent. 1	Revenues	6	229,000	
	Fund Balance	5		229,000
	To close revenues into			
	Fund Balance.			
Cl. Ent. 2	Fund Balance	5	204,500	
	Expenditures	7		204,500
	To close expenditures			
	into Fund Balance.			

CITY OF DOWDLE
GENERAL FUND
POSTCLOSING TRIAL BALANCE
December 31, 19X5

Closing	21,500	
Taxes Receivable	15,000	
Fund Balance		36,500
	36,500	36,500

SUMMARY EXAMPLE FOR CITY OF WINSTON

Further practice in the principles of fund accounting presented up to this point can be obtained by working the following problem for the City of Winston. An attempt should be made to complete the problem befor looking at the solution provided.

It should be noted that the accounts that were closed have been *ruled*. To avoid the possibility of combining the figures from one year with those of an ensuing year, the following procedure is followed:

1. A single ruling is drawn across the amount columns beneath the last figure in the longer of the two columns (the lines should be drawn on the same horizontal line in both columns).

2. The total of each column is written beneath the single rulings in normal-sized figures on the line (as opposed to pencil footings which are small and not placed on the line). These totals should be the same.

3. Double rulings are drawn beneath the totals across all columns except the item columns.

CITY OF WINSTON
GENERAL FUND

The operations of the General Fund of the City of Winston for the year ended December 31, 19X6, are summarized as follows:

The following balances were in the accounts at the beginning of the year:

Cash	$7,000
Fund Balance	$7,000

The transactions for the City of Winston for 19X6 were as follows:

1. The City levied property taxes of $120,000.
2. The City purchased material and supplies on credit for $45,000.
3. The City borrowed $50,000 in anticipation of collecting taxes.
4. The City received $65,000 from the payment of property taxes.
5. Payment was made for one-half of the materials and supplies purchased.
6. The City paid salaries of employees in the amount of $80,000.
7. The City paid $25,000 on its tax anticipation note liability.
8. The City collected the following:

Property Taxes	$50,000
Parking Meters	10,000
Issuance of Licenses	5,000

9. The City paid the following:

Vouchers Payable	$21,500
Tax Anticipation Notes	25,000

10. The City refunded $500 for an overassessment that had been paid by a taxpayer.

Requirements

1. **Make General Journal entries.**
2. **Post to accounts.**
3. **Prepare a trial balance.**
4. **Journalize and post closing entries.**
5. **Prepare postclosing trial balance.**

CITY OF WINSTON
GENERAL FUND
GENERAL JOURNAL

Date	Account Titles	Post Ref.	Debit	Credit
Tr. 1	Taxes Receivable	2	120,000.00	
	Revenues	6		120,000.00
	To record levy of property taxes.			
Tr. 2	Expenditures	7	45,000.00	
	Vouchers Payable	3		45,000.00
	To record preparation of voucher for materials and supplies.			
Tr. 3	Cash	1	50,000.00	
	Notes Payable	4		50,000.00
	To record bank loan on tax anticipation notes.			
Tr. 4	Cash	1	65,000.00	
	Taxes Receivable	2		65,000.00
	To record receipt of taxes previously accrued.			
Tr. 5	Vouchers Payable	3	22,500.00	
	Cash	1		22,500.00
	To record payment of voucher.			
Tr. 6	Expenditures	7	80,000.00	
	Vouchers Payable	3		80,000.00
	To reocrd preparation of voucher for salaries.			
	Vouchers Payable	3	80,000.00	
	Cash	1		80,000.00
	To record payment of voucher.			
Tr. 7	Notes Payable	4	25,000.00	
	Vouchers Payable	3		25,000.00
	To record preparation of voucher for note payable.			

Date	Account Titles	Post Ref.	Debit	Credit
	Vouchers Payable	3	25,000.00	
	Cash	1		25,000.00
	To record payment of voucher.			
Tr. 8	Cash	1	65,000.00	
	Taxes Receivable	2		50,000.00
	Revenues	6		15,000.00
	To record collection of taxes previously accrued and miscellaneous revenues.			
Tr. 9	Notes Payable	4	25,000.00	
	Vouchers Payable	3		25,000.00
	To record preparation of voucher for note payable.			
	Vouchers Payable	3	46,500.00	
	Cash	1		46,500.00
	To record payment of voucher.			
Tr. 10	Revenues	6	500.00	
	Vouchers Payable	3		500.00
	To record refund on over-assessment of taxes.			
	Vouchers Payable	3	500.00	
	Cash	1		500.00
	To record payment of voucher.			

CLOSING ENTRIES

Date	Account Titles	Post Ref.	Debit	Credit
Cl. Ent. 1	Revenues	6	134,500.00	
	Fund Balance	5		134,500.00
	To close revenues into fund balance.			

Date	Account Titles	Post Ref.	Debit	Credit
Cl. Ent. 2	Fund Balance	5	125,000.00	
	Expenditures	7		125,000.00
	To close expenditures into			
	fund balance.			

CITY OF WINSTON
GENERAL FUND
GENERAL LEDGER

Cash   Acct. No. 1

19X6							
Jan.	1 Balance	✓	7,000.00	Tr.	5	1	22,500.00
Tr.	3	1	50,000.00	Tr.	6	1	80,000.00
Tr.	4	1	65,000.00	Tr.	7	2	25,000.00
Tr.	8	2	65,000.00	Tr.	9	2	46,500.00
		12,500	*187,000.00*	Tr.	10	2	500.00
							174,000.00

Taxes Receivable   Acct. No. 2

Tr.	1	1	120,000.00	Tr.	4	1	65,000.00
				Tr.	8	2	50,000.00

Vouchers Payable   Acct. No. 3

Tr.	5	1	22,500.00	Tr.	2	1	45,000.00
Tr.	6	1	80,000.00	Tr.	6	1	80,000.00
Tr.	7	2	25,000.00	Tr.	7	1	25,000.00
Tr.	9	2	46,500.00	Tr.	9	2	25,000.00
Tr.	10	2	500.00	Tr.	10	2	500.00
			174,000.00			*1,000*	*175,500.00*

Notes Payable   Acct. No. 4

Tr.	7	1	25,000.00	Tr.	3	1	50,000.00
Tr.	9	2	25,000.00				
			50,000.00				

			Fund Balance			Acct. No. 5	
			19X6				
Cl. Ent. 2	2	125,000.00	Jan. 1 Balance		✓		7,000.00
			Cl. Ent. 1		2		134,500.00
				16,500			*141,500.00*

			Revenues			Acct. No. 6	
Tr. 10	2	500.00	Tr. 1		1	120,000.00	
Cl. Ent. 1	2	134,500.00	Tr. 8		2	15,000.00	
		135,000.00		*134,500*		135,000.00	

			Expenditures		Acct. No. 7	
Tr. 2	1	45,000.00	Cl. Ent. 2	2	125,000.00	
Tr. 6	1	80,000.00				
		125,000.00			125,000.00	

CITY OF WINSTON
GENERAL FUND
TRIAL BALANCE
December 31, 19X6

Cash	12,500.00	
Taxes Receivable	5,000.00	
Vouchers Payable		1,000.00
Fund Balance		7,000.00
Revenues		134,500.00
Expenditures	125,000.00	
	142,500.00	142,500.00

CITY OF WINSTON
GENERAL FUND
POSTCLOSING TRIAL BALANCE
December 31, 19X6

Cash	12,500.00	
Taxes Receivable	5,000.00	
Vouchers Payable		1,000.00
Fund Balance		16,500.00
	17,500.00	17,500.00

Problem 5-1

Use the transaction information given in Problem 4-1.

Requirements

1. Journalize and post closing entries.
2. Rule the accounts.
3. Prepare a postclosing trial balance.

Problem 5-2

Use the transaction information given in Problem 4-2.

Requirements

1. Journalize and post closing entries.
2. Rule the accounts.
3. Prepare a postclosing trial balance.

6

BUDGET ENTRY, ENCUMBRANCES, AND TAXES RECEIVABLE

THE BUDGET ENTRY

The estimated revenues and appropriations, in the amounts approved by the legislative body, are actually recorded on the books where they may be compared with the actual developments of the period. As soon as the appropriation ordinance is passed, an entry is made setting up estimated revenues and appropriations on the records.

Examples of budget entries:

1.	Estimated Revenues	110,000	
	Fund Balance		2,000
	Appropriations		108,000
	To record the budget (when estimated revenues exceed appropriations).		
2.	Estimated Revenues	120,000	
	Fund Balance	2,000	
	Appropriations		122,000
	To record the budget (when appropriations exceed estimated revenues).		

RECORDING ENCUMBRANCES

As the executive branch makes expenditures and commitments (called *encumbrances*) to make other expenditures, it reduces the amounts of appropriations available to authorize further expenditures and commitments. One of accounting's functions is to provide administrators with information regarding the current status of appropriations so that they will not exceed their spending authority. Conceptually the report takes the following form:

Appropriations	$ \quad X$
Expenditures	$-Y$
Unexpended Balance	$ \quad X - Y$
Encumbrances	$-Z$
Unencumbered Balance	$X - (Y + Z)$

In earlier chapters the maintenance of an Expenditures account was explained and illustrated. But it is also necessary to maintain a record of the estimated amount of proposed expenditures. As a purchase order is placed, an entry is made to record its amount as a debit in the Encumbrances account. As we have seen, the Encumbrances account encumbers (sets aside) a part of the Appropriations account. But nothing has really happened to the principal members of the accounting equation until the purchase order is filled (i.e., until the goods are received). Consequently, as the debit is made to the Encumbrances account—a memorandum, temporary fund balance account—a credit is made to the Reserve for Encumbrances account—also a memorandum, temporary fund balance account. The term "memorandum" is used because the accounts are offsetting in nature and the result is that information regarding outstanding purchase orders is available, but no essential change in the accounting equation has been made.

When the purchase order is filled by the arrival of goods, the amount of the expenditure is determined. It is nearly always indicated by an invoice from the supplier. The entry for the purchase order is then reversed, and the expenditure is recorded. The following transactions and entries illustrate the described sequence:

1. The purchase order is placed for $30,000.

Encumbrances	30,000	
Reserve for Encumbrances		30,000
To record placement of the purchase order.		

2. The goods are received, together with an invoice for $30,000.

    a. | | | |
    |---|---|---|
    | Reserve for Encumbrances | 30,000 | |
    | Encumbrances | | 30,000 |
    | To record reversal of the entry encumbering appropriations *in the amount of the purchase order.* | | |

b. Expenditures   30,000

    Vouchers Payable   30,000

  To record an expenditure *in the amount of the invoice.*

It is not unusual for the amount of the invoice to differ from the amount of the purchase order. Suppose that the amount of the invoice in the foregoing example had been $29,500 or $31,000 instead of $30,000. In either case entry 2a is made for the amount of the purchase order since its purpose is to remove the purchase order from outstanding status. Entry 2b would then be made for the amount of the invoice, which is the amount of the expenditure and the liability.

If the invoice amount is greater or smaller than the amount of the purchase order, the unencumbered balance of appropriations is changed. Suppose that the total appropriation for the above example is $100,000. The following schedule indicates the effects of three different invoice amounts on the unencumbered balance of appropriations:

	After Issuance of Purchase Order of $30,000	If Expenditure of $30,000	If Expenditure of $31,000	If Expenditure of $29,500
	Column 1	Column 2	Column 3	Column 4
Appropriation	100,000	100,000	100,000	100,000
Expenditures	-0-	30,000	31,000	29,500
Unexpended Balance	100,000	70,000	69,000	70,500
Encumbrances	30,000	-0-	-0-	-0-
Unencumbered Balance	70,000	70,000	69,000	70,500

Note that:

1. No matter what the amount of the invoice, the encumbrance amount (the amount of the purchase order) is wiped out when the purchase order is filled.

2. If the amount of the invoice is the same as the amount of the purchase order, as in column 2 and entries 2a and 2b, recording the expenditure *does not alter* the unencumbered balance.

3. If the amount of the invoice is greater than the amount of the purchase order, as in column 3, the unencumbered balance *is decreased* by the amount of the difference, $1,000.

4. If the amount of the invoice is less than the amount of the purchase order, as in column 4, the unencumbered balance *is increased* by the amount of the difference, $500.

Let us follow the same process assuming an order is placed for $500.00 and when it is received, the invoice is for $500.00. Further assume a second order is subsequently placed for $1,000.00 and when it is received the invoice amount is $975.00.

	Before Order No. 1	Order No. 1 Placed	Order No. 1 Received	Order No. 2 Placed	Order No. 2 Received
Appropriations	10,000	10,000	10,000	10,000	10,000
Less: Expenditures	-0-	-0-	500	500	1,475
Unexpended Balance	10,000	10,000	9,500	9,500	8,525
Less: Encumbrances	-0-	500	-0-	1,000	-0-
Unencumbered Balance	10,000	9,500	9,500	8,500	8,525

The sequence of entries for the transactions involving Orders No. 1 and No. 2 would have been as follows:[1]

Order No. 1

Encumbrances	500	
Reserve for Encumbrances		500
Reserve for Encumbrances	500	
Encumbrances		500
Expenditures	500	
Vouchers Payable		500
Vouchers Payable	500	
Cash		500

Order No. 2

Encumbrances	1,000	
Reserve for Encumbrances		1,000
Reserve for Encumbrances	1,000	
Encumbrances		1,000
Expenditures	975	
Vouchers Payable		975
Vouchers Payable	975	
Cash		975

TAXES RECEIVABLE

The entry to record the tax levy as previously presented was as follows:

Taxes Receivable	50,000	
Revenues		50,000

---

[1] Explanation will be omitted to conserve space.

Taxes are the most important revenues of the general funds of cities and usually the first to accrue. It is, however, unrealistic to assume that all of the taxes will be collected. Using past experience and estimates of future economic conditions, governments may estimate that a certain percentage of the taxes will be uncollectible, although at the time of the levy, it is not known which particular or individual taxes will not be collected.

Assume that a tax levy of $50,000 is made and that it is estimated that 5 percent of the taxes will be uncollectible. The following entry will then be made:

Taxes Receivable	50,000	
Estimated Uncollectible Taxes		2,500
Revenues		47,500

The estimated uncollectible taxes are ordinarily treated as a direct reduction from revenue, as in the preceding entry. The estimated uncollectible account may be referred to as a contra account. A contra account is defined as an account that partially or wholly offsets another.

At such time as it becomes known that a specific account (for example, one for $2,000) is uncollectible, the following entry is made:

Estimated Uncollectible Taxes	2,000	
Taxes Receivable		2,000

After these two entries are posted, the Taxes Receivable account and the Estimated Uncollectible Taxes account would look like this:

Taxes Receivable			Estimated Uncollectible Taxes	
50,000	2,000		2,000	2,500
48,000				500

Each time taxes are paid, cash is debited and taxes receivable is credited. Assume $47,000 of the above taxes have been paid, and the $47,000 has been posted to the Taxes Receivable account.

Taxes Receivable			Estimated Uncollectible Taxes	
50,000	2,000		2,000	2,500
1,000	47,000			500
	49,000			

It may happen that the estimate made for uncollectible taxes will prove to be incorrect. Assume that the entry to record the tax levy was as follows:

Taxes Receivable	76,000	
Estimated Uncollectible Taxes		1,000
Revenues		75,000

Assume further that collections of $75,200 are made:

| Cash | 75,200 | |
| Taxes Receivable | | 75,200 |

If these entries were posted to the ledger, the T-accounts would appear as follows:

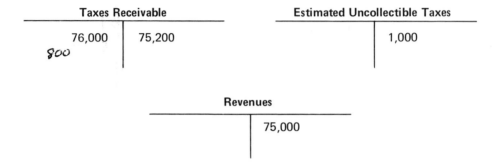

| **Taxes Receivable** | | **Estimated Uncollectible Taxes** | |
| 76,000 *800* | 75,200 | | 1,000 |

| **Revenues** | |
| | 75,000 |

Note that the balance in the Estimated Uncollectible Taxes account exceeds that of Taxes Receivable. Since it is incorrect to show a greater amount that is uncollectible than that which is available for collection, an adjusting entry must be made. The entry to be made must at least reduce the Estimated Uncollectible Taxes account to an amount equal to that of the balance in the Taxes Receivable account. The following entry is made:

| Estimated Uncollectible Taxes | 200 | |
| Revenues | | 200 |

The Revenues account is credited because in the original entry to record the tax levy the city overestimated the amount that would prove to be uncollectible and thereby understated the amount to be credited to Revenues.

Taxes receivable may be further identified as Taxes Receivable—Current, being those taxes that were levied in the current year, and as Taxes Receivable—Delinquent, being those that were not collected in the year in which they were levied and therefore were transferred with the following entry:

| Taxes Receivable—Delinquent | |
| Taxes Receivable—Current | |

In addition, the related contra asset accounts must also be transferred:

| Estimated Uncollectible Taxes—Current | |
| Estimated Uncollectible Taxes—Delinquent | |

Some other transactions that involve taxes receivable or revenues related to taxes receivable are given below:

1. Taxpayer is overassessed but error is discovered before payment is made by taxpayer.

    Revenues
    > Taxes Receivable—Current

    (Note: As a practical matter, no change will be made in the Estimated Uncollectible Taxes—Current at this time; as the uncollectible account is simply an estimate, any changes can be made at the end of the year with an adjusting entry if necessary.)

2. Taxpayer is overassessed but the error is not discovered until after taxpayer has sent in payment.

    Revenues
    > Vouchers Payable

    Vouchers Payable
    > Cash

3. Taxpayer is assessed correctly but inadvertently sends in an overpayment.

    Taxes Receivable—Current
    > Vouchers Payable

    Vouchers Payable
    > Cash

To understand the rationale behind any correction, it is a good practice to reconstruct the original entry which created the error and analyze what must be done to effect the desired change.

EXAMPLE OF CLOSING ENTRIES INCORPORATING NEW ACCOUNTS

Closing entries will be discussed in more detail in the next chapter, but it is desirable at this point to expand on the closing entries already presented to include the budgetary accounts introduced in this chapter. Closing entry one will consist of a debit to Revenues, a credit to Estimated Revenues, with the balancing amount debited or credited to Fund Balance. Closing entry two will consist of a debit to Appropriations, a credit to Expenditures, with the balancing amount debited or credited to Fund Balance. The examples below use fabricated figures for the purpose of illustration:

C1-1	Revenues	100,000	
	Fund Balance	7,000	
	Estimated Revenues		107,000

(Note: Had the Revenues figure exceeded the Estimated Revenues figure, Fund Balance would have been credited.)

C1-2	Appropriations	105,000	
	Fund Balance		3,000
	Expenditures		102,000

(Note: Had the Expenditures exceeded Appropriations, Fund Balance would have been debited.)

Problem 6-1

CITY OF EDGEMONT
GENERAL FUND

Beginning balances of the General Fund of the City of Edgemont at December 31, 19X4, were as follows:

Cash	2,000	
Taxes Receivable—Current	2,000	
Estimated Uncollectible		
Taxes—Current		100
Vouchers Payable		900
Fund Balance		3,000
	4,000	4,000

1. Taxes Receivable—Current that are not collected by December 31, 19X3, become delinquent as of January 1, 19X4.
2. Revenues were estimated at $200,000. Appropriations of $197,000 were made.
3. Property taxes were levied in the amount of $150,000. It is estimated that 1 percent of these taxes will not be collected.
4. An order was placed for materials estimated to cost $25,200.
5. The materials were received, and the actual cost was $25,000.
6. Citizens paid $130,000 of taxes, of which $1,000 was payment of delinquent taxes.
7. The City received $50,000 of miscellaneous revenue.
8. The voucher for the materials (Transaction 5) and the beginning balance in Vouchers Payable were paid.
9. Salaries were paid in the amount of $120,000.
10. Materials and supplies were ordered at an estimated cost of $30,000.
11. Materials and supplies were received at an actual cost of $31,000.
12. Office equipment was ordered at an estimated cost of $20,000.
13. The City wrote off $100 of delinquent taxes as uncollectible.
14. Office equipment was received at an actual cost of $20,300.
15. Vouchers were paid in the amount of $31,000.
16. The City received $14,000 in payment of property taxes.

Requirements

1. Enter the beginning trial balance in ledger accounts.
2. Prepare General Journal entries for all transactions.
3. Post to the ledger.
4. Prepare a trial balance.
5. Prepare closing entries.
6. Prepare a postclosing trial balance.

Problem 6-2

CITY OF FREEMONT
GENERAL FUND

Beginning balances of the General Fund of the City of Freemont at January 1, 19X5, were as follows:

Cash	2,000	
Taxes Receivable—Delinquent	4,000	
Estimated Uncollectible Taxes—Delinquent		300
Vouchers Payable		2,700
Fund Balance		3,000
	6,000	6,000

1. Revenues were estimated at $350,000. Appropriations of $351,000 were made.
2. Property taxes were levied in the amount of $325,000. It is estimated that 3 percent of these taxes will not be collected.
3. An order was placed for materials estimated to cost $21,000.
4. The materials were received, and the actual cost was $25,000.
5. $230,000 was received from citizens in payment of taxes, of which $2,000 was payment of delinquent taxes.
6. $20,000 of miscellaneous revenue was received.
7. The voucher for the materials (Transaction 4) and the beginning balance in Vouchers Payable were paid.
8. Salaries were paid in the amount of $120,000.
9. Materials and supplies were ordered at an estimated cost of $45,000.
10. Materials and supplies were received at an actual cost of $42,500.
11. Office equipment was ordered at an estimated cost of $20,000.
12. $200 of delinquent taxes was written off as uncollectible.
13. Office equipment was received at an actual cost of $20,150.
14. All outstanding vouchers were paid.

15. $80,000 was received in payment of property taxes.

16. Current taxes not collected become delinquent as of December 31, 19X5.

Requirements

1. **Journalize.**
2. **Post.**
3. **Prepare a trial balance.**
4. **Journalize and post closing entries.**
5. **Prepare a postclosing trial balance.**

7

CLOSING ENTRIES EXPANDED

CLOSING ENTRIES EXPANDED FOR
REVENUE ACCOUNTS

When estimated revenues exceed actual revenues, the closing entry for revenues takes the following form:

Revenues	428,700	
Fund Balance	2,300	
Estimated Revenues		431,000

When actual revenues exceed estimated revenues, the closing entry takes the following form:

Revenues	435,000	
Estimated Revenues		431,000
Fund Balance		4,000

The revenue closing entry must close the Estimated Revenues and Revenues accounts and transfer the difference, whether debit or credit, to Fund Balance. In this process the estimate of revenues, credited to Fund Balance when the budget was recorded at the beginning of the year, is adjusted so that the net credit to the Fund Balance account is the amount of the actual revenue.

CLOSING ENTRIES EXPANDED FOR
EXPENDITURE ACCOUNTS

The procedure for closing expenditure and related accounts is determined by the legal provisions of the government pertaining to the lapsing of appropriations and to related matters affecting the expenditure for an article purchased in one year but ordered in a preceding year. An appropriation is said to lapse when it terminates, that is, when it may no longer be used as authorization to make an expenditure.

The closing entries for expenditure accounts then may take several different forms; in this text two will be illustrated. These two have been arbitrarily designated *Assumption A* and *Assumption B* by the authors for ease in presentation.

ASSUMPTION A.   Under Assumption A encumbered appropriations do not lapse; the closing entry should leave on the books the Reserve for Encumbrances account, which becomes the authorization for the purchase of the encumbered article in the year or years following the year of appropriation.

The closing entry for expenditures under Assumption A would be as follows:

Appropriations	426,000	
Expenditures		399,900
Encumbrances		20,000
Fund Balance		6,100

This entry compares Appropriations with Expenditures and Encumbrances, closes those accounts, and converts the Reserve for Encumbrances from a memorandum account to a reservation of fund balance. A reservation of fund balance represents a portion of the fund balance that is not available for appropriation. Under Assumption A, in the next period the Reserve for Encumbrances will serve as authorization for the expenditure of amounts encumbered prior to year end. (See the next two entries.) It will therefore function as an appropriation—an appropriation approved by the legislative body in the prior year and carried forward through the mechanism of the preceding closing entry.

To begin the next year of operations under Assumption A, it is necessary to make the following entry (this entry should be the first entry of the new year):

Reserve for Encumbrances	20,000	
Reserve for Encumbrances—		
Prior Years		20,000
To set up the Reserve for Encumbrances account carried forward from the preceding year		

in a separate account so as to
distinguish it from the Reserve
for Encumbrances account applicable to the current year.

As expenditures that are authorized by the Reserve for Encumbrances—Prior Years are
incurred during the year, they are debited to an account called Expenditures Chargeable to
Reserve for Encumbrances—Prior Years. For example, assume that the items represented by the
Reserve for Encumbrances account in a preceding illustration ($20,000) are received during the
next fiscal year at an actual cost of $19,500. The following entry would be made to record this
transaction:

Expenditures Chargeable to RE—PY	19,500	
Vouchers Payable		19,500

Note the distinction between the two accounts Expenditures and Expenditures Chargeable to
Reserve for Encumbrances—Prior Years. The Expenditures Chargeable to RE—PY will exist
only under Assumption A.

When using Assumption A, there are three closing entries to be made rather than the two
that are necessary when using Assumption B. The third closing entry under Assumption A
closes out the Reserve for Encumbrances—Prior Years and the Expenditures Chargeable to
Reserve for Encumbrances—Prior Years with any difference going into Fund Balance as follows:

Reserve for Encumbrances—PY	20,000	
Expenditures Chargeable to RE—PY		19,500
Fund Balance		500

ASSUMPTION B.   Under Assumption B encumbered appropriations lapse; the
closing entry for expenditures will close out both the Reserve for Encumbrances and the
Encumbrances accounts (these memorandum accounts will have identical balances in them).

The closing entry for expenditures under Assumption B would be as follows:

Appropriations	426,000	
Reserve for Encumbrances	20,000	
Expenditures		399,900
Encumbrances		20,000
Fund Balance		26,100

See Figure 1 for a complete summary of the closing entries for both Assumptions A and B.

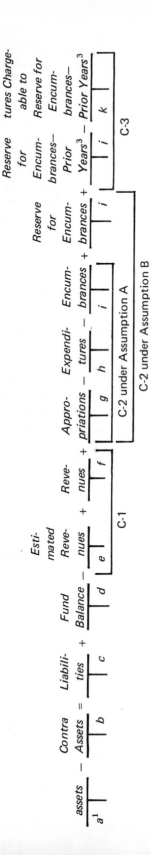

C-1
A & B[2]

	Debit	Credit
Revenues	f	
Estimated Revenues		e
Fund Balance		f − e

To close the revenue accounts if Revenues exceed Estimated Revenues. If f < e, Fund Balance would be debited with e − f.

C-2
A

	Debit	Credit
Appropriations	g	
Expenditures		h
Encumbrances		i
Fund Balance		g − (h + i)

To close the current year expenditure accounts. Since the sum of expenditures and encumbrances normally may not exceed appropriations, there will seldom be a debit to Fund Balance. The Reserve for Encumbrances account is not closed.

C-2
B

	Debit	Credit
Appropriations	g	
Reserve for Encumbrances	i	
Expenditures		h
Encumbrances		i
Fund Balance		$g - h$

To close the expenditure accounts. Note that the credit to Fund Balance in this entry exceeds that in C-2 under Assumption A by the amount i of orders outstanding at year end.

C-3
A

	Debit	Credit
Reserve for Encumbrances—Prior Years	j	
Expenditures Chargeable to Reserve for Encumbrances—Prior Years		k
Fund Balance		$j - k$

To close the prior year expenditure accounts. Since the expenditures normally may not exceed the authorizations, there will seldom be a debit to Fund Balance.

Notes:

[1] Lower case letters represent dollar balances in the accounts at the time the preclosing trial balance is prepared.

[2] "A" and "B" refer to the assumptions stated in Chapter 7 of the text.

[3] The accounts Reserve for Encumbrances—Prior Years and Expenditures Chargeable to Reserve for Encumbrances—Prior Years are used only under Assumption A.

FIGURE 1

Closing Entries—Assumptions A and B.

A more detailed illustration of the transactions involved under Assumptions A and B follows in Figures 2 and 3. The accounts and amounts used in the illustration are based on the trial balance provided for "A Governmental Unit." Only those entries that relate to the closing process are presented.

We recommend that the student prepare two ledgers, one for each assumption, and post the entries in the Figures to these ledgers. The differences may then be identified by comparison of the accounts in the two ledgers.

A GOVERNMENTAL UNIT
GENERAL FUND
TRIAL BALANCE
December 31, 19X0

	Debit	Credit
Cash	11,200	
Taxes Receivable—Delinquent	69,000	
Estimated Uncollectible Delinquent Taxes		11,000
Interest and Penalties Receivable on Taxes	550	
Estimated Uncollectible Interest and Penalties		50
Accounts Receivable	21,000	
Estimated Uncollectible Accounts		1,000
Vouchers Payable		29,900
Due to Working Capital Fund		30,000
Taxes Collected in Advance		1,000
Reserve for Encumbrances, 19X0		20,000
Fund Balance		5,000
Estimated Revenues, 19X0	431,000	
Revenues, 19X0		428,700
Appropriations, 19X0		426,000
Expenditures, 19X0	399,900	
Encumbrances, 19X0	20,000	
	952,650	952,650

Note: The temporary fund balance accounts have been dated to emphasize the sources of authority to spend. The dating renders unnecessary the entry that converts the Reserve for Encumbrances to the Reserve for Encumbrances—Prior Years.

FIGURE 2
A governmental unit—trial balance.

A GOVERNMENTAL UNIT
GENERAL FUND
SUMMARY OF APPROPRIATION-EXPENDITURE ACCOUNTING

	Assumption A		Assumption B	
December 31, 19X0:	Debit	Credit	Debit	Credit
Appropriations, 19X0	426,000		426,000	
Reserve for Encumbrances, 19X0			20,000	
Expenditures, 19X0		399,900		399,900
Encumbrances, 19X0		20,000		20,000
Fund Balance		6,100		26,100
To record the closing of accounts related to appropriations.				
January 1, 19X1:				
Fund Balance	444,000		464,000	
Appropriations, 19X1		444,000		464,000
To record the budget for the second year.				
Encumbrances, 19X1			20,000	
Reserve for Encumbrances, 19X1				20,000
To record as encumbrances of the second year the orders placed but not filled in the first year.				
Transactions, 19X1:				
Encumbrances, 19X1	220,000		220,000	
Reserve for Encumbrances, 19X1		220,000		220,000
To record reduction of appropriations by amount of estimated cost of purchase orders placed.				
Reserve for Encumbrances, 19X1	205,000		225,000	
Encumbrances, 19X1		205,000		225,000
To reverse the entry encumbering Appropriations.				
Expenditures, 19X1	418,000		437,500	
Vouchers Payable		418,000		437,500
To record expenditures and the resulting liability.				

	Assumption A		Assumption B	
	Debit	Credit	Debit	Credit
Expenditures Chargeable to				
Reserve for Encumbrances, 19X0	19,500			
Vouchers Payable		19,500		
To record expenditures and the resulting liability.				
December 31, 19X1:				
Appropriations, 19X1	444,000		464,000	
Reserve for Encumbrances, 19X1			15,000	
Expenditures, 19X1		418,000		437,500
Encumbrances, 19X1		15,000		15,000
Fund Balance		11,000		26,500
To close appropriations, expenditures and encumbrances of 19X1.				
Reserve for Encumbrances, 19X0	20,000			
Expenditures Chargeable to				
Reserve for Encumbrances, 19X0		19,500		
Fund Balance		500		
To close accounts relating to orders first placed in 19X0.				

FIGURE 3

A governmental unit—summary of appropriation-expenditure accounting.

MAKING ASSUMPTIONS FROM YEAR-END BALANCES

At the end of each year the postclosing trial balance contains the balances in the accounts of the General Ledger for the beginning of the new year. The solution of problems in fund accounting frequently requires that conclusions be drawn from a year-end trial balance as to the type of closing entries that were made and, hence, as to the legal provisions governing such entries.

For example, the presence in a postclosing trial balance of Reserve for Encumbrances indicates that encumbered appropriations do not lapse (Assumption A) and that expenditures incurred as a result of the purchase orders represented in the Reserve for Encumbrances account are to be charged to the Expenditures Chargeable to Reserve for Encumbrances—PY account in the new year. When the postclosing trial balance indicates the presence of a Reserve for Encumbrances, the first entry of the new year should be:

Reserve for Encumbrances
    Reserve for Encumbrances—Prior Years

In the absence of a clear indication of a change of legal provisions, the operating and closing entries should be prepared using the assumption that was used in the preparation of the previous year's closing entries.

Similarly, the absence of accounts for current taxes from a year-end postclosing trial balance means that taxes become delinquent before the end of the year and that the balances of Taxes Receivable—Current and Estimated Uncollectible Taxes—Current should be transferred before year-end to their delinquent counterparts without the need for a "transaction" that gives such direction.

SUMMARY EXAMPLES FOR ASSUMPTION A AND B PROBLEMS

The following examples (City W and City D) illustrate the concepts covered up to this point. City W is prepared under Assumption A; City D is prepared under Assumption B. Both of these problems and their solutions should be carefully studied before working the problems in this chapter.

CITY W
GENERAL FUND

The trial balance of the General Fund of City W on January 1, 19X0, was as follows:

CITY W
GENERAL FUND
TRIAL BALANCE
January 1, 19X0

Cash	15,000	
Taxes Receivable—Delinquent	20,000	
Estimated Uncollectible Taxes—		
Delinquent		3,000
Interest and Penalties Receivable		
on Taxes	1,000	
Estimated Uncollectible Interest		
and Penalties		75
Accounts Receivable	10,000	
Estimated Uncollectible Accounts		1,000
Vouchers Payable		20,500
Reserve for Encumbrances—Prior Years		10,000
Fund Balance		11,425
	46,000	46,000

The following are transactions that took place during the year 19X0:

1. Revenues were estimated at $110,000; appropriations of $108,000 were made.
2. An order placed at the end of the preceding year and estimated to cost $10,000 was received; the invoice indicated an actual cost of $9,500.
3. Taxes to the amount of $110,000 have accrued; an allowance of 5 percent was made for possible losses.
4. Collections were made as follows:

Current Taxes	$90,000
Delinquent Taxes	10,000
Interest and Penalties Receivable on Taxes	300
Accounts Receivable	5,000

5. Taxes amounting to $20,000 have become delinquent; the allowance for uncollectible current taxes was transferred to the allowance for uncollectible delinquent taxes.
6. Delinquent taxes amounting to $2,000 were written off; interest and penalties receivable on taxes to the amount of $20 were also written off.
7. An order was placed for materials estimated to cost $20,000.
8. Delinquent taxes amounting to $200, which were written off in preceding years, were collected with interest and penalties of $35.
9. Payments were made as follows:

Vouchers Payable	$15,500
Payrolls	20,000

10. The materials ordered were received; a bill for $21,000 was also received.
11. An order was placed for an automobile for the police department; the estimated cost was $3,000.
12. Payrolls of $25,000 were paid.
13. The automobile ordered for the police department was received; the actual cost was $3,000.
14. Bonds to the amount of $10,000 have matured.
15. The matured bonds were paid.
16. Interest amounting to $5,000 was paid.
17. Interest of $600 accrued on delinquent taxes, and an allowance for uncollectible losses thereon of 5 percent was provided.
18. An order was placed for materials estimated to cost $19,000.

Requirements

1. **Post the opening trial balance to T-accounts.**

2.   Prepare journal entries.
3.   Post to T-accounts.
4.   Prepare closing entries.
5.   Post to T-accounts.
6.   Prepare postclosing trial balance.

CITY W
GENERAL FUND
GENERAL JOURNAL

Page 1

Date	Account Titles	Post Ref.	Debit	Credit
Tr. 1	Estimated Revenues	13	110,000.00	
	Fund Balance	12		2,000.00
	Appropriations	15		108,000.00
	To record the budget.			
Tr. 2	Expenditures Chargeable to RE—PY	19	9,500.00	
	Vouchers Payable	10		9,500.00
	To record preparation of voucher for prior year expenditures.			
Tr. 3	Taxes Receivable—Current	2	110,000.00	
	Estimated Uncollect- ible Taxes—Current	3		5,500.00
	Revenues	14		104,500.00
	To record the tax levy.			
Tr. 4	Cash	1	105,300.00	
	Taxes Receivable— Current	2		90,000.00
	Taxes Receivable— Delinquent	4		10,000.00
	Interest and Penalties Receivable on Taxes	6		300.00
	Accounts Receivable	8		5,000.00
	To record collections.			
Tr. 5	Taxes Receivable—Delinquent	4	20,000.00	
	Taxes Receivable— Current	2		20,000.00
	To record change in status of taxes receivable.			
	Estimated Uncollectible Taxes—Current	3	5,500.00	
	Estimated Uncollect- ible Taxes—Delinquent	5		5,500.00
	To record change in status of estimated uncollectible accounts.			

Date	Account Titles	Post Ref.	Debit	Credit
Tr. 6	Estimated Uncollectible Taxes—Delinquent	5	2,000.00	
	Estimated Uncollectible Interest and Penalties	7	20.00	
	Taxes Receivable— Delinquent	4		2,000.00
	Interest and Penalties Receivable	6		20.00
	To record the writing off of amounts termed uncollectible.			
Tr. 7	Encumbrances	17	20,000.00	
	Reserve for Encumbrances	18		
	To record encumbrance for materials.			20,000.00
Tr. 8	Cash	1	235.00	
	Revenues	14		235.00
	To record collection of taxes previously written off.			
Tr. 9	Expenditures	16	20,000.00	
	Vouchers Payable	10		20,000.00
	To record preparation of voucher.			
	Vouchers Payable	10	35,500.00	
	Cash	1		35,500.00
	To record payment of voucher.			
Tr. 10	Reserve for Encumbrances	18	20,000.00	
	Encumbrances	17		20,000.00
	To record cancellation of encumbrance.			
	Expenditures	16	21,000.00	
	Vouchers Payable	10		21,000.00
	To record preparation of voucher.			

Date	Account Titles	Post Ref.	Debit	Credit
Tr. 11	Encumbrances	17	3,000.00	
	Reserve for			
	Encumbrances	18		3,000.00
	To record encumbrance for automobile.			
Tr. 12	Expenditures	16	25,000.00	
	Vouchers Payable	10		25,000.00
	To record preparation of voucher.			
	Vouchers Payable	10	25,000.00	
	Cash	1		25,000.00
	To record payment of voucher.			
Tr. 13	Reserve for Encumbrances	18	3,000.00	
	Encumbrances	17		3,000.00
	To record cancellation of encumbrance.			
	Expenditures	16	3,000.00	
	Vouchers Payable	10		3,000.00
	To record preparation of voucher for automobile.			
Tr. 14	Expenditures	16	10,000.00	
	Matured Bonds Payable	11		10,000.00
	To record matured bonds.			
Tr. 15	Matured Bonds Payable	11	10,000.00	
	Vouchers Payable	10		10,000.00
	To record preparation of voucher for bond payable.			
	Vouchers Payable	10	10,000.00	
	Cash	1		10,000.00
	To record payment of voucher.			

Date	Account Titles	Post Ref.	Debit	Credit
Tr. 16	Expenditures	16	5,000.00	
	Vouchers Payable	10		5,000.00
	To record preparation of voucher.			
	Vouchers Payable	10	5,000.00	
	Cash	1		5,000.00
	To record payment of voucher.			
Tr. 17	Interest and Penalties Receivable on Taxes	6	600.00	
	Estimated Uncollectible Interest and Penalties	7		30.00
	Revenues	14		570.00
	To record accruing of interest.			
Tr. 18	Encumbrances	17	19,000.00	
	Reserve for Encumbrances	18		19,000.00
	To record encumbrance for materials.			

CLOSING ENTRIES

Date	Account Titles	Post Ref.	Debit	Credit
Cl. Ent. 1	Revenues	14	105,305.00	
	Fund Balance	12	4,695.00	
	Estimated Revenues	13		110,000.00
	To close revenues accounts			
	into fund balance.			
Cl. Ent. 2	Appropriations	15	108,000.00	
	Expenditures	16		84,000.00
	Encumbrances	17		19,000.00
	Fund Balance	12		5,000.00
	To close expenditure accounts			
	into fund balance.			
Cl. Ent. 3	Reserve for Encumbrances— PY	20	10,000.00	
	Expenditures Charge- able to RE—PY	19		9,500.00
	Fund Balance	12		500.00
	To close prior year accounts			
	into fund balance.			

CITY W
GENERAL FUND
GENERAL LEDGER

Cash   Acct. No. 1

19X0							
Jan.	1 Balance	✓	15,000.00	Tr.	9	2	35,500.00
Tr.	4	1	105,300.00	Tr.	12	3	25,000.00
Tr.	8	2	235.00	Tr.	15	3	10,000.00
			43,035 /20,535.00	Tr.	16	4	5,000.00
							75,500.00

Taxes Receivable—Current   Acct. No. 2

Tr.	3	1	110,000.00	Tr.	4	1	90,000.00
				Tr.	5	1	20,000.00
			110,000.00				110,000.00

Estimated Uncollectible Taxes—Current   Acct. No. 3

Tr.	5	1	5,500.00	Tr.	3	1	5,500.00

Taxes Receivable—Delinquent   Acct. No. 4

19X0							
Jan.	1 Balance	✓	20,000.00	Tr.	4	1	10,000.00
Tr.	5	1	20,000.00	Tr.	6	2	2,000.00
		28,000	*40,000.00*				*12,000.00*

Estimated Uncollectible Taxes—Delinquent   Acct. No. 5

Tr.	6	2	2,000.00	19X0			
				Jan.	1 Balance	✓	3,000.00
				Tr.	5	1	5,500.00
						6,500	*8,500.00*

Interest and Penalties Receivable on Taxes   Acct. No. 6

19X0							
Jan.	1 Balance	✓	1,000.00	Tr.	4	1	300.00
Tr.	17	4	600.00	Tr.	6	2	20.00
		1,280	*1,600.00*				*320.00*

Estimated Uncollectible Interest and Penalties   Acct. No. 7

Tr.	6	2	20.00	19X0			
				Jan.	1 Balance	✓	75.00
				Tr.	17	4	30.00
						85.00	*105.00*

Accounts Receivable   Acct. No. 8

19X0							
Jan.	1 Balance	✓	10,000.00	Tr.	4	1	5,000.00
			5,000.00				

Estimated Uncollectible Accounts Receivable   Acct. No. 9

				19X0			
				Jan.	1 Balance	✓	1,000.00

Vouchers Payable — Acct. No. 10

					19X0				
Tr.	9	2	35,500.00		Jan.	1	Balance	✓	20,500.00
Tr.	12	3	25,000.00		Tr.	2		1	9,500.00
Tr.	15	3	10,000.00		Tr.	9		2	20,000.00
Tr.	16	4	5,000.00		Tr.	10		2	21,000.00
			75,500.00		Tr.	12		3	25,000.00
					Tr.	13		3	3,000.00
					Tr.	15		3	10,000.00
					Tr.	16		4	5,000.00
								38,500	*114,000.00*

Matured Bonds Payable — Acct. No. 11

Tr.	15	3	10,000.00	Tr.	14	3	10,000.00

Fund Balance — Acct. No. 12

					19X0				
Cl. Ent.	1	4	4,695.00		Jan.	1	Balance	✓	11,425.00
					Tr.	1		1	2,000.00
					Cl. Ent.	2		5	5,000.00
					Cl. Ent.	3		5	500.00
								14,230	*18,925.00*

Estimated Revenues — Acct. No. 13

Tr.	1	1	110,000.00	Cl. Ent.	1	5	110,000.00

Revenues — Acct. No. 14

Cl. Ent.	1	5	105,305.00	Tr.	3	1	104,500.00
				Tr.	8	2	235.00
				Tr.	17	4	570.00
			105,305.00				105,305.00

Appropriations — Acct. No. 15

Cl. Ent.	2	5	108,000.00	Tr.	1	1	108,000.00

Expenditures   Acct. No. 16

Tr.	9	2	20,000.00	Cl. Ent.	2		5	84,000.00
Tr.	10	2	21,000.00					
Tr.	12	3	25,000.00					
Tr.	13	3	3,000.00					
Tr.	14	3	10,000.00					
Tr.	16	4	5,000.00					
			84,000.00					84,000.00

Encumbrances   Acct. No. 17

Tr.	7	2	20,000.00	Tr.	10		2	20,000.00
Tr.	11	3	3,000.00	Tr.	13		3	3,000.00
Tr.	18	4	19,000.00	Cl. Ent.	2		5	19,000.00
			42,000.00					42,000.00

Reserve for Encumbrances   Acct. No. 18

Tr.	10	2	20,000.00	Tr.	7		2	20,000.00
Tr.	13	3	3,000.00	Tr.	11		3	3,000.00
			23,000.00	Tr.	18		4	19,000.00
						19,000		*42,000.00*

Expenditures Chargeable to Reserve for Encumbrances—PY   Acct. No. 19

Tr.	2	1	9,500.00	Cl. Ent.	3		5	9,500.00

Reserve for Encumbrances—PY   Acct. No. 20

				19X0				
Cl. Ent.	3	5	10,000.00	Jan.	1	Balance	✓	10,000.00

CITY W
GENERAL FUND
TRIAL BALANCE
December 31, 19X0

Cash	45,035.00	
Taxes Receivable—Delinquent	28,000.00	
Estimated Uncollectible Taxes— Delinquent		6,500.00
Interest and Penalties Receivable on Taxes	1,280.00	
Estimated Uncollectible Interest and Penalties		85.00
Accounts Receivable	5,000.00	
Estimated Uncollectible Accounts		1,000.00
Vouchers Payable		38,500.00
Fund Balance		13,425.00
Estimated Revenues	110,000.00	
Revenues		105,305.00
Appropriations		108,000.00
Expenditures	84,000.00	
Encumbrances	19,000.00	
Reserve for Encumbrances		19,000.00
Expenditures Chargeable to RE—PY	9,500.00	
Reserve for Encumbrances—PY		10,000.00
	301,815.00	301,815.00

CITY W
GENERAL FUND
POSTCLOSING TRIAL BALANCE
December 31, 19X0

Cash	45,035.00	
Taxes Receivable—Delinquent	28,000.00	
Estimated Uncollectible Taxes— Delinquent		6,500.00
Interest and Penalties Receivable on Taxes	1,280.00	
Estimated Uncollectible Interest and Penalties		85.00
Accounts Receivable	5,000.00	
Estimated Uncollectible Accounts Receivable		1,000.00
Vouchers Payable		38,500.00
Fund Balance		14,230.00
Reserve for Encumbrances		19,000.00
	79,315.00	79,315.00

CITY D
GENERAL FUND

The following is a trial balance of the General Fund of City D as of December 31, 19X0, after closing entries (interest and penalties on taxes are not accrued):

CITY D
GENERAL FUND
TRIAL BALANCE
December 31, 19X0

Cash	33,600	
Taxes Receivable—Delinquent	25,400	
Estimated Uncollectible Taxes—		
Delinquent		5,900
Accounts Receivable	15,500	
Estimated Uncollectible Accounts		2,500
Vouchers Payable		42,000
Fund Balance		24,100
	74,500	74,500

The following transactions took place during 19X1:

1. The budget for the year was adopted. Revenues were estimated at $216,000; appropriations of $229,000 were made, including an appropriation of $16,000 for materials ordered in 19X0, covered by the Reserve for Encumbrances.

2. The materials ordered in 19X0 and set up as an encumbrance of that year for $16,000 were received; the actual cost was $15,000.

3. Delinquent taxes amounting to $2,800 were declared uncollectible and written off the books.

4. Taxes to the amount of $210,000 accrued; a 3 percent allowance for estimated losses was provided.

5. Uniforms estimated to cost $15,000 were ordered.

6. Collections were made as follows:

Current taxes	$182,000
Delinquent taxes	8,500
Interest and penalties on taxes	200
Accounts receivable	7,300

7. Interest of $3,000 was paid.

8. Payroll vouchers for $100,000 were approved.

9. The uniforms were received; the invoice was for $16,000.

10.   Serial bonds to the amount of $35,000 matured.

11.   Delinquent taxes to the amount of $350, written off in preceding years, were collected.

12.   Current taxes became delinquent; the amount of estimated uncollectible current taxes was transferred to estimated uncollectible delinquent taxes.

13.   The payroll vouchers were paid.

14.   An order was placed for a snow plow estimated to cost $3,500.

15.   Vouchers paid amounted to $60,000.

16.   The snow plow was received; the invoice was for $3,800.

17.   Matured serial bonds were retired.

18.   Miscellaneous revenues of $5,000 were collected.

19.   An order was placed for civil defense equipment at an estimated cost of $24,000.

Requirements

1.   **Post the opening trial balance to T-accounts.**

2.   **Prepare journal entries.**

3.   **Post to accounts.**

4.   **Prepare closing entries.**

5.   **Post closing entries to accounts.**

6.   **Prepare postclosing trial balance.**

CITY D
GENERAL FUND
GENERAL JOURNAL

Page 1

Date	Account Titles	Post Ref.	Debit	Credit
Tr. 1	Estimated Revenues	11	216,000.00	
	Fund Balance	10	13,000.00	
	Appropriations	13		229,000.00
	To record the budget entry.			
	Encumbrances	15	16,000.00	
	Reserve for Encumbrances	16		16,000.00
	To record portion of appropriation that is encumbered.			
Tr. 2	Reserve for Encumbrances	16	16,000.00	
	Encumbrances	15		16,000.00
	To record cancellation of encumbrance.			
	Expenditures	14	15,000.00	
	Vouchers Payable	8		15,000.00
	To record preparation of voucher.			
Tr. 3	Estimated Uncollectible Taxes—Delinquent	5	2,800.00	
	Taxes Receivable—Delinquent	4		2,800.00
	To record write-off of uncollectible taxes.			
Tr. 4	Taxes Receivable—Current	2	210,000.00	
	Estimated Uncollectible Taxes—Current	3		6,300.00
	Revenues	12		203,700.00
	To record tax levy.			
Tr. 5	Encumbrances	15	15,000.00	
	Reserve for Encumbrances	16		15,000.00
	To record encumbrance for uniforms.			

Date	Account Titles	Post Ref.	Debit	Credit
Tr. 6	Cash	1	198,000.00	
	Taxes Receivable— Current	2		182,000.00
	Taxes Receivable— Delinquent	4		8,500.00
	Revenues	12		200.00
	Accounts Receivable	6		7,300.00
	To record collections.			
Tr. 7	Expenditures	14	3,000.00	
	Vouchers Payable	8		3,000.00
	To record preparation of voucher for interest.			
	Vouchers Payable	8	3,000.00	
	Cash	1		3,000.00
	To record payment of voucher.			
Tr. 8	Expenditures	14	100,000.00	
	Vouchers Payable	8		100,000.00
	To record preparation of voucher for payroll.			
Tr. 9	Reserve for Encumbrances	16	15,000.00	
	Encumbrances	15		15,000.00
	To record cancellation of encumbrance.			
	Expenditures	14	16,000.00	
	Vouchers Payable	8		16,000.00
	To record preparation of voucher for uniforms.			
Tr. 10	Expenditures	14	35,000.00	
	Matured Bonds Payable	9		35,000.00
	To record maturing of serial bonds.			
Tr. 11	Cash	1	350.00	
	Revenues	12		350.00
	To record collection of taxes previously written off.			

Date	Account Titles	Post Ref.	Debit	Credit
Tr. 12	Taxes Receivable—Delinquent	4	28,000.00	
	Estimated Uncollectible			
	Taxes—Current	3	6,300.00	
	Taxes Receivable—			
	Current	2		28,000.00
	Estimated Uncollectible			
	Taxes—Delinquent	5		6,300.00
	To record change of status			
	in taxes receivable.			
Tr. 13	Vouchers Payable	8	100,000.00	
	Cash	1		100,000.00
	To record payment of			
	payroll vouchers.			
Tr. 14	Encumbrances	15	3,500.00	
	Reserve for			
	Encumbrances	16		3,500.00
	To record encumbrance for			
	snow plow ordered.			
Tr. 15	Vouchers Payable	8	60,000.00	
	Cash	1		60,000.00
	To record payment of			
	vouchers outstanding.			
Tr. 16	Reserve for Encumbrances	16	3,500.00	
	Encumbrances	15		3,500.00
	To record cancellation of			
	encumbrance.			
	Expenditures	14	3,800.00	
	Vouchers Payable	8		3,800.00
	To record voucher for snow			
	plow.			
Tr. 17	Matured Bonds Payable	9	35,000.00	
	Vouchers Payable	8		35,000.00
	To record preparation of			
	voucher.			
	Vouchers Payable	8	35,000.00	
	Cash	1		35,000.00
	To record payment of			
	voucher.			

Date	Account Titles	Post Ref.	Debit	Credit
Tr. 18	Cash	1	5,000.00	
	Revenues	12		5,000.00
	To record collection of miscellaneous revenues.			
Tr. 19	Encumbrances	15	24,000.00	
	Reserve for Encumbrances	16		24,000.00
	To record encumbrance for civil defense equipment.			

CLOSING ENTRIES

Date	Account Titles	Post Ref.	Debit	Credit
Cl. Ent. 1	Revenues	12	209,250.00	
	Fund Balance	10	6,750.00	
	Estimated Revenues	11		216,000.00
	To close revenues accounts			
	into fund balance.			
Cl. Ent. 2	Reserve for Encumbrances	16	24,000.00	
	Appropriations	13	229,000.00	
	Encumbrances	15		24,000.00
	Expenditures	14		172,800.00
	Fund Balance	10		56,200.00
	To close expenditures			
	accounts into fund balance.			

CITY D
GENERAL FUND
GENERAL LEDGER

Cash   Acct. No. 1

19X1							
Jan.	1 Balance	✓	33,600.00	Tr.	7	2	3,000.00
Tr.	6	2	198,000.00	Tr.	13	3	100,000.00
Tr.	11	2	350.00	Tr.	15	3	60,000.00
Tr.	18	4	5,000.00	Tr.	17	3	35,000.00
	38,950		*236,950.00*				*198,000.00*

Taxes Receivable—Current   Acct. No. 2

Tr.	4	1	210,000.00	Tr.	6	2	182,000.00
				Tr.	12	3	28,000.00
			210,000.00				210,000.00

Estimated Uncollectible Taxes—Current   Acct. No. 3

Tr.	12	3	6,300.00	Tr.	4	1	6,300.00

Taxes Receivable—Delinquent   Acct. No. 4

19X1								
Jan.	1 Balance	✓	25,400.00	Tr.	3	1	2,800.00
Tr.	12	3	28,000.00	Tr.	6	2	8,500.00
	42,100	*53,400.00*					*11,300.00*

Estimated Uncollectible Taxes—Delinquent   Acct. No. 5

				19X1			
Tr.	3	1	2,800.00	Jan.	1 Balance	✓	5,900.00
				Tr.	12	3	6,300.00
					9,400		*12,200.00*

Accounts Receivable   Acct. No. 6

19X1							
Jan.	1 Balance	✓	15,500.00	Tr.	6	2	7,300.00
	8,200						

Estimated Uncollectible Accounts Receivable   Acct. No. 7

		19X1			
		Jan.	1 Balance	✓	2,500.00

Vouchers Payable   Acct. No. 8

				19X1			
Tr.	7	2	3,000.00	Jan.	1 Balance	✓	42,000.00
Tr.	13	3	100,000.00	Tr.	2	1	15,000.00
Tr.	15	3	60,000.00	Tr.	7	2	3,000.00
Tr.	17	3	35,000.00	Tr.	8	2	100,000.00
		198,000.00		Tr.	9	2	16,000.00
				Tr.	16	3	3,800.00
				Tr.	17	3	35,000.00
					16,800		*214,800.00*

Matured Bonds Payable   Acct. No. 9

Tr.	17	3	35,000.00	Tr.	10	2	35,000.00

			Fund Balance				**Acct. No. 10**
				19X1			
Tr.	1	1	13,000.00	Jan.	1 Balance	✓	24,100.00
Cl. Ent.	1	5	6,750.00	Cl. Ent.	2	5	56,200.00
			19,750.00			*60,550*	*80,300.00*

			Estimated Revenues				**Acct. No. 11**
Tr.	1	1	216,000.00	Cl. Ent.	1	5	216,000.00

			Revenues				**Acct. No. 12**
Cl. Ent.	1	5	209,250.00	Tr.	4	1	203,700.00
				Tr.	6	2	200.00
				Tr.	11	2	350.00
				Tr.	18	4	5,000.00
			209,250.00				209,250.00

			Appropriations				**Acct. No. 13**
Cl. Ent.	2	5	229,000.00	Tr.	1	1	229,000.00

			Expenditures				**Acct. No. 14**
Tr.	2	1	15,000.00	Cl. Ent.	2	5	172,800.00
Tr.	7	2	3,000.00				
Tr.	8	2	100,000.00				
Tr.	9	2	16,000.00				
Tr.	10	2	35,000.00				
Tr.	16	3	3,800.00				
			172,800.00				172,800.00

			Encumbrances				**Acct. No. 15**
Tr.	1	1	16,000.00	Tr.	2	1	16,000.00
Tr.	5	1	15,000.00	Tr.	9	2	15,000.00
Tr.	14	3	3,500.00	Tr.	16	3	3,500.00
Tr.	19	4	24,000.00	Cl. Ent.	2	5	24,000.00
			58,500.00				58,500.00

Reserve for Encumbrances   Acct. No. 16

Tr.	2	1	16,000.00	Tr.	1	1	16,000.00
Tr.	9	2	15,000.00	Tr.	5	1	15,000.00
Tr.	16	3	3,500.00	Tr.	14	3	3,500.00
Cl. Ent.	2	5	24,000.00	Tr.	19	4	24,000.00
			58,500.00				58,500.00

CITY D
GENERAL FUND
TRIAL BALANCE
December 31, 19X1

Cash	38,950.00	
Taxes Receivable—Delinquent	42,100.00	
Estimated Uncollectible Taxes—		
Delinquent		9,400.00
Accounts Receivable	8,200.00	
Estimated Uncollectible Accounts		
Receivable		2,500.00
Vouchers Payable		16,800.00
Fund Balance		11,100.00
Estimated Revenues	216,000.00	
Revenues		209,250.00
Appropriations		229,000.00
Expenditures	172,800.00	
Encumbrances	24,000.00	
Reserve for Encumbrances		24,000.00
	502,050.00	502,050.00

CITY D GENERAL FUND
POSTCLOSING TRIAL BALANCE
December 31, 19X1

Cash	38,950.00	
Taxes Receivable—Delinquent	42,100.00	
Estimated Uncollectible Taxes—		
Delinquent		9,400.00
Accounts Receivable	8,200.00	
Estimated Uncollectible Accounts		
Receivable		2,500.00
Vouchers Payable		16,800.00
Fund Balance		60,550.00
	89,250.00	89,250.00

Problem 7-1

CITY OF ZEN
GENERAL FUND

The trial balance of the General Fund of the City of Zen on January 1, 19X6, was as follows:

CITY OF ZEN
GENERAL FUND
TRIAL BALANCE
January 1, 19X6

Cash	10,000	
Taxes Receivable—Delinquent	25,000	
Estimated Uncollectible Taxes—		
Delinquent		4,000
Interest and Penalties Receivable		
on Taxes	500	
Estimated Uncollectible Interest		
and Penalties		25
Accounts Receivable	5,000	
Estimated Uncollectible Accounts		500
Vouchers Payable		15,000
Reserve for Encumbrances—PY		11,000
Fund Balance		9,975
	40,500	40,500

The following transactions took place during the year 19X6:

1. Revenues were estimated at $165,000; appropriations of $160,000 were made.
2. Taxes of $165,000 accrued, and an allowance of 4 percent was made for possible losses.
3. Collections were made as follows:

Current taxes	$140,000
Delinquent taxes	15,000
Interest and penalties	
receivable on taxes	200
Accounts receivable	3,000

4. An order placed at the end of the preceding year and estimated to cost $11,000 was received; the invoice indicates an actual cost of $10,000.
5. The unpaid portion of the 19X6 tax levy became delinquent; the allowance for

uncollectible current taxes was transferred to the allowance for uncollectible delinquent taxes.

6. An order was placed for materials estimated to cost $25,000.

7. Payments were made as follows:

Vouchers Payable	$13,000
Payrolls	30,000

8. Delinquent taxes amounting to $4,000 were written off; interest and penalties receivable on taxes of $15 were also written off.

9. The materials ordered in Transaction 6 were received; a bill for $27,000 was also received.

10. Delinquent taxes of $500, which were written off in preceding years, were collected with interest and penalties of $50.

11. An order was placed for a new fire truck; the estimated cost was $45,000.

12. Payroll vouchers of $25,000 were approved.

13. Serial bonds of $30,000 matured.

14. An order was placed for materials estimated to cost $1,500.

15. The fire truck ordered was received; the actual cost was $44,000.

16. The matured bonds were paid.

17. Interest of $400 accured on delinquent taxes, and an allowance for uncollectible losses thereon of 5 percent was provided.

18. Interest amounting to $2,000 was paid.

19. Miscellaneous revenues of $4,000 were collected.

20. The payroll vouchers were paid; other vouchers of $44,000 were also paid.

Requirements

1. **Record the opening trial balance in T-accounts.**
2. **Prepare journal entries.**
3. **Post to T-accounts.**
4. **Prepare a preclosing trial balance.**
5. **Prepare closing entries.**
6. **Post closing entries to T-accounts.**
7. **Prepare postclosing trial balance.**

Problem 7-2

CITY MN
GENERAL FUND

The following is a list of account balances of the General Fund of City MN on December 31, 19X7:

CITY MN
GENERAL FUND
TRIAL BALANCE
December 31, 19X7

Cash	20,000	
Taxes Receivable—Delinquent	25,000	
Estimated Uncollectible Taxes— Delinquent		1,000
Interest and Penalties Receivable on Taxes	500	
Estimated Uncollectible Interest and Penalties		20
Vouchers Payable		23,000
Reserve for Encumbrances		11,000
Fund Balance		10,480
	45,500	45,500

The following is a summary of transactions for 19X8:

1. Revenues were estimated at $150,000; appropriations of $145,000 were made.
2. Taxes of $150,000 accrued; an allowance of 5 percent was made for possible losses.
3. The only order outstanding at the end of the preceding year was received; invoice was received in the amount of $10,000.
4. Collections were made as follows:

Current taxes	120,000
Delinquent taxes	15,000
Interest and penalties receivable on taxes	200
Miscellaneous revenue	3,000
	$138,200

5. Taxes of $30,000 have become delinquent; the estimated uncollectable current taxes were transferred to the estimated uncollectible delinquent taxes.
6. An order was placed for materials estimated to cost $50,000.
7. Delinquent taxes of $3,000 were written off.
8. Delinquent taxes of $500, written off in a preceding year, were collected with interest and penalties of $50.
9. The following payments were made:

| Vouchers Payable | $20,000 |
| Payrolls | 40,000 |

10. The material ordered in Transaction 6 was received; the related invoice for $48,000 was also received.

11. Bonds of $8,000 have matured.

12. An order was placed for materials estimated to cost $35,000.

13. The matured bonds were paid.

14. Interest of $200 accrued on delinquent taxes; an allowance of 5 percent was made for losses.

15. Payments were made as follows:

| Interest | $10,000 |
| Vouchers Payable | 50,000 |

Requirements

1. **Record the opening trial balance in T-accounts.**
2. **Prepare journal entries.**
3. **Post to T-accounts.**
4. **Prepare a preclosing trial balance.**
5. **Prepare closing entries.**
6. **Post to T-accounts.**
7. **Prepare a postclosing trial balance.**

Problem 7-3

VILLAGE OF OLAN
GENERAL FUND

The following is a trial balance of the General Fund of the Village of Olan as of December 31, 19X3, after closing entries have been posted:

VILLAGE OF OLAN
GENERAL FUND
TRIAL BALANCE
December 31, 19X3

Cash	3,400	
Taxes Receivable—Delinquent	7,800	
Estimated Uncollectible Taxes—		
Delinquent		3,900
Due to Stores Fund		550
Vouchers Payable		2,600
Fund Balance		4,150
	11,200	11,200

The following transactions took place during 19X4:

1. The budget for the year was adopted. Revenues were estimated at $187,000; appropriations of $183,500 were made, including an appropriation of $6,750 for materials ordered in 19X3, covered by the Reserve for Encumbrances.
2. The amount owed to the Stored Fund was paid.
3. Taxes in the amount of $180,000 accrued; a 2.5 percent estimate was provided for estimated uncollectibles.
4. The materials ordered in 19X3 were received; the invoice amount was $6,950.
5. Collections were made as follows:

Current taxes	$173,000
Delinquent taxes	2,500
Interest and penalties receivable on taxes	110
Miscellaneous revenue	50

6. Interest of $2,000 was paid.
7. Delinquent taxes amounting to $1,300 were declared uncollectible and written off.
8. An order was placed for equipment estimated to cost $15,900.
9. Payroll vouchers for $72,000 were approved.
10. Serial bonds in the amount of $50,000 matured.
11. The equipment previously ordered was received; the invoice amount was for $17,530.
12. All outstanding vouchers were paid including any established in the prior year.
13. Serial bonds were paid.
14. Miscellaneous revenues were collected in the amount of $6,200.
15. An order was placed for office equipment in the amount of $950.
16. Delinquent taxes in the amount of $180, written off in a preceding year, were collected.

17.   A voucher was prepared to reimburse taxpayer overassessed in the amount of $350. (Taxpayer had already sent in payment before error was discovered.)

18.   Supplies were received from the Stores Fund in the amount of $400.

Requirements

1.   Enter beginning balances in the General Ledger.
2.   Journalize and post transactions.
3.   Prepare a trial balance.
4.   Journalize and post closing entries.
5.   Prepare a postclosing trial balance.

8

FINANCIAL STATEMENTS

Although coverage of financial statements is handled primarily by the principal text, this chapter is included for the purpose of providing further examples. When studying the examples here and those in the principal text, close attention should be paid to contrasts, particularly with regard to the Analysis of Changes in Fund Balance statement.

In the event that the beginning balance in the Fund Balance account (which is the starting point in preparing the Analysis of Changes in Fund Balance statement), is not known but you do know the preclosing trial balance figure for Fund Balance, it is possible to compute the beginning balance in Fund Balance with the following equation (assume the Fund Balance account balance on preclosing trial balance is $11,100):

Beginning Balance (X)	+	Estimated Revenues	−	Appropriations	=	Fund Balance on Preclosing Trial Balance
X	+	216,000	−	229,000	=	11,100
X		−	13,000		=	11,100
				X	=	24,100

ANALYSIS OF CHANGES IN FUND BALANCE STATEMENT

Figure 4 is an example of an Analysis of Changes in Fund Balance. Location of the several comparisons (e.g., in the Deduct category: "Excess of estimated revenues over revenues") is determined by the effect of the comparison on fund balance. For example, if revenues exceed estimated revenues, the comparison goes in the Add category; if estimated revenues exceed revenues, the comparison goes in the Deduct category.

A GOVERNMENTAL UNIT
GENERAL FUND
ANALYSIS OF CHANGES IN FUND BALANCE
For the Year Ending December 31, 19X1

Fund balance, January 1, 19X1			$8,800
Add:			
Excess of estimated revenues over appropriations:			
Estimated revenues		$450,000	
Appropriations		$444,000	6,000
Excess of appropriations over expenditures and encumbrances:			
Appropriations		444,000	
Expenditures	$418,000		
Encumbrances	15,000	433,000	11,000
Excess of reserve for excumbrances, 19X0, over expenditures chargeable thereto:			
Reserve for Encumbrances, 19X0		$20,000	
Expenditures chargeable thereto		19,500	500
			$26,300
Deduct:			
Excess of estimated revenues over revenues:			
Estimated revenues		$450,000	
Revenues		446,000	4,000
Fund balance, December 31, 19X1			$22,300

FIGURE 4
A governmental unit—analysis of changes in fund balance.

EXAMPLE OF THE ANALYSIS OF CHANGES IN FUND BALANCE AND BALANCE SHEET PREPARED UNDER ASSUMPTIONS A AND B

The following trial balance figures are the basis for examples of financial statements under Assumptions A and B. As the problem is presented, the City has been operating under Assumption A (Figures 5 and 6), and the Assumption A statements are prepared on that basis.

In preparing the Assumption B statements (Figures 7 and 8), it is assumed that all spending authorities and expenditures remain the same—that the only change is in the law governing the lapsing of appropriations.

The data are provided under Assumption A. To use the same data for an Assumption B solution, the two accounts that do not exist under Assumption B (Expenditures Chargeable to Reserve for Encumbrances—Prior Years and Reserve for Encumbrances—Prior Years) must be deleted and incorporated into two other accounts as follows:

1. The balance of Expenditures Changeable to Reserve for Encumbrances—Prior years is added to Expenditures resulting in a new balance in Expenditures.
2. The balance of Reserve for Encumbrances—Prior Years is added to Appropriations resulting in a new Appropriations figure.

This exercise is provided for pedagogical purposes. Rarely would the preparation of Assumption B statements be based on Assumption A data.

CITY OF YUMA
GENERAL FUND
TRIAL BALANCE
December 31, 19X4

Cash	6,500	
Taxes Receivable—Deliquent	30,000	
Estimated Uncollectible Taxes—Delinquent		4,000
Accounts Receivable	10,000	
Estimated Uncollectible Accounts		1,000
Vouchers Payable		22,000
Due to Intragovernmental Service Fund		3,000
Reserve for Encumbrances—Prior Years		5,000
Reserve for Encumbrances		12,000
Fund Balance		13,400
Estimated Revenues	400,000	
Revenues		385,000
Appropriations		420,000
Expenditures	402,000	
Encumbrances	12,000	
Expenditures Chargeable to Reserve for Prior Years	4,900	
	865,400	865,400

ASSUMPTION A

X +	Estimated Revenues	− Appropriations	=	Fund Balance on Preclosing Trial Balance
X +	400,000	− 420,000	=	13,400
		X − 20,000	=	13,400
		X	=	33,400

ASSUMPTION B

X +	Estimated Revenues	− Appropriations	=	Fund Balance on Preclosing Trial Balance
X +	400,000	− 425,000	=	13,400
		X − 25,000	=	13,400
		X	=	38,400

Assumption A

CITY OF YUMA
GENERAL FUND
ANALYSIS OF CHANGES IN FUND BALANCE
For the Year Ending December 31, 19X4

Fund balance, January 1, 19X4			$33,400
Add:			
Excess of appropriations over expenditures and encumbrances:			
Appropriations		$420,000	
Expenditures	$402,000		
Encumbrances	12,000	414,000	6,000
Excess of reserve for encumbrances—prior year over expenditures chargeable to reserve for encumbrances—prior year:			
Reserve for encumbrances—PY		$5,000	
Expenditures chargeable to RE—PY		4,900	100
			$39,500

Deduct:
Excess of estimated
  revenues over revenues:

Estimated revenues	$400,000		
Revenues	385,000	$15,000	

Excess of appropriations over
  estimated revenues:

Appropriations	$420,000		
Estimated revenues	400,000	20,000	35,000

Fund balance, December 31, 19X4			$4,500

FIGURE 5
City of Yuma—analysis of changes in fund balance.

Assumption A

CITY OF YUMA
GENERAL FUND
BALANCE SHEET
December 31, 19X4

Assets

Cash		$6,500
Taxes receivable—delinquent	$30,000	
Less: Estimated uncollectible taxes—		
delinquent	4,000	26,000
Accounts receivable	$10,000	
Less: Estimated uncollectible		
accounts receivable	1,000	9,000
Total assets		$41,500

Liabilities, reserves, and fund balance

Liabilities:		
Vouchers payable	$22,000	
Due to Intragovernmental Service Fund	3,000	$25,000
Reserve for encumbrances		12,000
Fund balance		4,500
Total libailities, reserves, and fund balance		
		$41,500

FIGURE 6
City of Yuma—balance sheet.

Assumption B

CITY OF YUMA
GENERAL FUND
ANALYSIS OF CHANGES IN FUND BALANCE
For the Year Ending December 31, 19X4

Fund balance, January 1, 19X4			$38,400
Add:			
Excess of appropriations			
over expenditures:			
Appropriations		$425,000	
Expenditures		406,900	18,100
			$56,500
Deduct:			
Excess of appropriations			
over estimated revenues:			
Appropriations	$425,000		
Estimated Revenues	400,000	$25,000	
Excess of estimated			
revenues over revenues:			
Estimated revenues	$400,000		
Revenues	385,000	15,000	40,000
Fund balance, December 31, 19X4			$16,500

FIGURE 7
City of Yuma—analysis of changes in fund balance.

Assumption B

CITY OF YUMA
GENERAL FUND
BALANCE SHEET
December 31, 19X4

Assets

Cash		$6,500
Taxes receivable—delinquent	$30,000	
Less: Estimated uncollectible taxes— delinquent	4,000	26,000
Accounts receivable	$10,000	
Less: Estimated uncollectible accounts receivable	1,000	9,000
Total assets		$41,500
Liabilities and fund balance		
Liabilities:		
Vouchers payable	$22,000	
Due to Intragovernmental Service Fund	3,000	$25,000
Fund balance		16,500
Total liabilities and fund balance		$41,500

FIGURE 8
City of Yuma—balance sheet.

Problem 8-1

CITY E
GENERAL FUND

The following information is from a preclosing trial balance of the General Fund of City E dated December 31, 19X3:

Cash	$20,000
Taxes Receivable	15,000
Estimated Uncollectible Taxes	1,000
Vouchers Payable	13,000
Reserve for Encumbrances—Prior Years	6,000
Reserve for Encumbrances	7,000
Fund Balance	20,900
Estimated Revenues	100,000
Revenues	90,000
Appropriations	105,000
Expenditures	95,000
Encumbrances	7,000
Expenditures Chargeable to Reserve for Encumbrances—Prior Years	5,900

Requirements

1. Prepare closing entries, December 31, 19X3.
2. Prepare a detailed analysis of changes in fund balance for the year ending December 31, 19X3.
3. Prepare a postclosing balance sheet as of December 31, 19X3.
4. Prepare a detailed analysis of changes in fund balance for the year ending December 31, 19X3, on the assumption that all facts are as given in the trial balance except that the City has always operated under a law that specified that all appropriations lapse as of the end of the year for which they are made.

Problem 8-2

CITY F
GENERAL FUND

The following information is from the preclosing trial balance of the General Fund of City F dated December 31, 19X3:

Cash	$15,000
Taxes Receivable	10,000
Estimated Uncollectible Taxes	1,000
Vouchers Payable	9,000
Reserve for Encumbrances, 19X2	4,000
Reserve for Encumbrances	4,000
Fund Balance	5,800
Estimated Revenues	120,000
Revenues	122,000
Appropriations	125,000
Expenditures	118,000
Encumbrances	4,000
Expenditures Chargeable to Reserve for	
for Encumbrances, 19X2	3,800

Requirements

1. Prepare closing entries, December 31, 19X3.
2. Prepare a detailed analysis of changes in fund balance for the year ending December 31, 19X3.
3. Prepare a postclosing balance sheet as December 31, 19X3.
4. Prepare a detailed analysis of changes in fund balance for the year ending December 31, 19X3, on the assumption that all facts are as given in the trial balance except that the City has always operated under a law that specified that all appropriations lapse as of the end of the year for which they are made.

Problem 8-3

CITY OF WA
GENERAL FUND
TRIAL BALANCE
December 31, 19X0

Cash	45,035	
Taxes Receivable—Delinquent	30,000	
Estimated Uncollectible Taxes—Delinquent		6,500
Interest and Penalties Receivable on Taxes	2,280	
Estimated Uncollectible Interest and Penalties		85
Accounts Receivable	5,000	
Estimated Uncollectible Accounts Receivable		1,000
Vouchers Payable		41,500
Reserve for Encumbrances—Prior Years		12,000
Reserve for Encumbrances		21,000
Fund Balance		13,425
Estimated Revenues	120,000	

Revenues		105,305
Appropriations		118,000
Expenditures	84,000	
Encumbrances	21,000	
Expenditures Chargeable Against Reserve for Encumbrances—Prior Years	11,500	
	318,815	318,815

Requirements

1. Prepare closing entries, December 31, 19X0.
2. Prepare a postclosing balance sheet as of December 31, 19X0.
3. Prepare an analysis of changes in fund balance for the year ending December 31, 19X0.

Problem 8-4

CITY OF WB
GENERAL FUND
TRIAL BALANCE
December 31, 19X0

Cash	45,035	
Taxes Receivable—Delinquent	28,000	
Estimated Uncollectible Taxes—Delinquent		6,500
Interest and Penalties Receivable on Taxes	1,280	
Estimated Uncollectible Interest and Penalties		85
Accounts Receivable	5,000	
Estimated Uncollectible Accounts Receivable		1,000
Vouchers Payable		38,500
Reserve for Encumbrances—Prior Years		10,000
Reserve for Encumbrances		19,000
Fund Balance		13,425
Estimated Revenues	110,000	
Revenues		105,305
Appropriations		108,000
Expenditures	84,000	
Encumbrances	19,000	
Expenditures Chargeable Against Reserve for Encumbrances—Prior Years	9,500	
	301,815	301,815

Requirements

1. Prepare closing entries, December 31, 19X0.
2. Prepare a postclosing balance sheet as of December 31, 19X0.

3.   Prepare an analysis of changes in fund balance for the year ending December 31, 19X0.

Problem 8-5

CITY OF EAZY
GENERAL FUND
PRECLOSING TRIAL BALANCE
December 31, 19X7

Cash	9,550	
Taxes Receivable—Delinquent	16,000	
Estimated Uncollectible		
Delinquent Taxes		7,000
Interest and Penalties Receivable		
on Taxes	500	
Estimated Uncollectible		
Interest and Penalties		25
Accounts Receivable	4,000	
Estimated Uncollectible Accounts		1,500
Estimated Revenues	200,000	
Appropriations		195,000
Expenditures Chargeable Against		
Reserve for Encumbrances—		
Prior Years	19,000	
Expenditures	188,000	
Vouchers Payable		20,000
Encumbrances	6,000	15,000
Reserve for Encumbrances		6,000
Fund Balance		8,000
Revenues		190,525
	443,050	443,050

Requirements

1.   Prepare closing entries, December 31, 19X0
2.   Prepare a postclosing balance sheet as of December 31, 19X7.
3.   Prepare an analysis of changes in fund balance for the year ending December 31, 19X7.

Problem 8-6

CITY OF DAVID
GENERAL FUND

The following is a trial balance of the General Fund of the City of David as of December 31, 19X6, after closing entries (interest and penalties on taxes are not accrued):

CITY OF DAVID
GENERAL FUND
TRIAL BALANCE
December 31, 19X6

Cash	20,000	
Taxes Receivable—Delinquent	23,000	
Estimated Uncollectible		
Taxes—Delinquint		4,000
Accounts Receivable	14,000	
Estimated Uncollectible Accounts		2,000
Vouchers Payable		41,000
Fund Balance		10,000
	57,000	57,000

The following transactions took place during 19X7:

1. Revenues were estimated at $300,000; appropriations of $310,000 were made, including an appropriation of $20,000 for materials ordered in 19X6.
2. Delinquint taxes of $3,000 were determined to be uncollectible and were written off the books.
3. The materials ordered in 19X6 were received; the actual cost was $18,000.
4. Taxes to the amount of $300,000 have accrued; a 1 percent allowance for estimated losses was provided.
5. Materials estimated to cost $25,000 were ordered.
6. Collections were made as follows:

Current Taxes	$240,000
Delinquent Taxes	10,000
Interest and Penalties on Taxes	500
Accounts Receivable	5,000
	$255,500

7. Payroll vouchers of $110,000 were approved.
8. Expenditures of $5,000 were incurred and paid.
9. Bonds of $40,000 have matured.
10. The materials ordered were received; the invoice was for $27,000.
11. Delinquent taxes of $500, written off in preceding years, were collected.
12. The payroll vouchers were paid.
13. Current taxes of $50,000 were collected.
14. Current taxes became delinquent; the amount of estimated uncollectible current taxes was transferred to estimated uncollectible delinquent taxes.

15. The matured bonds were retired.
16. Vouchers paid amounted to $50,000.
17. Miscellaneous revenues of $3,000 were collected.
18. Materials estimated to cost $20,000 were ordered.
19. Payrolls of $100,000 were paid.

Requirements

1. **Record the opening trial balance in the T-accounts.**
2. **Prepare journal entries for the transactions.**
3. **Post to T-accounts.**
4. **Prepare a trial balance.**
5. **Prepare closing entries.**
6. **Post closing entries to T-accounts.**
7. **Prepare a balance sheet as of December 31, 19X7.**
8. **Prepare an analysis of changes in fund balance for the year ended December 31, 19X7.**

9

SUBSIDIARY LEDGERS

In order to provide more detail regarding accounts such as Taxes Receivable, Accounts Receivable, Revenues, and Expenditures, it is customary to maintain special ledgers called *subsidiary ledgers*. The Revenues Subsidiary Ledger contains individual revenue accounts such as Property Taxes and Licenses so that it can be seen exactly how much revenue is received from each source; the Expenditures Subsidiary Ledger contains individual accounts such as Salaries and Materials and Supplies for principal organization units. For each subsidiary ledger a control account or accounts must be maintained in the General Ledger. The balance of the control account or accounts must always agree with the total of the balances of the accounts in the subsidiary ledger that it controls. Therefore, each time an amount is posted to the control account or accounts in the General Ledger, a like amount must be posted to an account or accounts in the subsidiary ledger. This procedure is illustrated in the sample problems for this chapter.

REVENUE ACCOUNTS

Separate General Ledger control accounts are established for estimated and actual revenues; that is, accounts entitled Estimated Revenues and Revenues are used. Two corresponding subsidiary ledgers with the titles of Estimated Revenues Subsidiary Ledger and Revenues Subsidiary Ledger might also be established. However, it is desirable, both from the standpoint of economy (fewer accounts are needed) and from the standpoint of ease of comparison of actual and estimated revenues, to record each estimated and actual revenue in the *same* subsidiary ledger account. Therefore, a single ledger, Revenues Subsidiary Ledger, is used to support the two control accounts, Estimated Revenues and Revenues. For example, the account for Property Tax Revenues would appear as follows in the Revenues Subsidiary Ledger:

Property Tax Revenues

Date	Description	Post. Ref.	Estimated Debit	Actual Credit	Balance Debit

As the estimates are set up, they are recorded in the Estimated Debit column. Subsequently, as revenues are accrued (or realized), the amount is entered in the Actual Credit column. A debit balance in an individual revenue account always indicates an excess of estimated revenue over actual revenue; a credit balance (indicated with parentheses or brackets: < >) indicates an excess of actual revenue over estimated revenue.

Revenue accounts are classified in order to produce information in a form useful to management in (1) preparing and controlling the budget, (2) controlling revenue, (3) preparing financial statements, and (4) preparing financial statistics. A classification of revenue accounts by source of revenue provides the necessary data for all of these purposes. The individual accounts set up will be determined by the needs of the particular state or municipality. Some of the revenue accounts that might be used are Property Taxes; Licenses and Permits; Fines, Forfeits, and Other Penalties; and Parking Meter Revenue.

EXPENDITURE ACCOUNTS

Three separate accounts—namely, Appropriations, Expenditures, and Encumbrances—are the control accounts in the General Ledger for the Expenditures Subsidiary Ledger. The individual account in the Expenditures Subsidiary Ledger will be comprised of each of these three elements (again, to provide the advantages of economy and ease of comparison) rather than setting up three separate expenditures subsidiary ledgers to handle appropriations, expenditures, and encumbrances for each individual expenditure account. An example of the form for an expenditure account is given below.

Fire Department Supplies

Date	Description	Reference Voucher No.	Reference Order No.	Encumbrances Created Debit	Encumbrances Liquidated Credit	Expenditures Debit	Appropriations Credit	Balance Credit

GENERAL LEDGER

+	−

Assets:
Cash
Taxes Receivable—Current
Taxes Receivable—Delinquent
Interest and Penalties Receivable
Accounts Receivable

Estimated Revenues

Expenditures
Encumbrances

Expenditures Chargeable
To Reserve for Encumbrances—Prior Years

GENERAL LEDGER

−	+

Contra Assets:
Estimated Uncollectible Taxes—Current
Estimated Uncollectible Taxes—Delinquent
Estimated Uncollectible Interest and Penalties
Estimated Uncollectible Accounts Receivable

Liabilities:
Vouchers Payable
Due to Working Capital Fund
Notes Payable
Taxes Collected in Advance
Fund Balance:
Fund Balance
Reserve for Encumbrances
Reserve for Encumbrances—Prior Years
Reserve for Inventory

Revenues

Appropriations

REVENUES LEDGER:
Property Taxes
Income Taxes
Interest and Penalties on Taxes
Motor Vehicle Licenses
Parking Meters
Municipal Court Fines
Interest on Bank Deposits

EXPENDITURES LEDGER:
Regular Salaries and Wages
Temporary Salaries and Wages
Other Personal Services
Printing
Electricity
Janitor Supplies
Clothing
Record Supplies
Rent
Surety Bond Premiums
Office Equipment

FIGURE 8
Typical Accounts

This form of account is invaluable to the finance officer in controlling appropriations. Regulations are set up providing that no purchase order or contract is valid unless it is approved by the finance officer. As an order is approved, the amount is entered in the Encumbrances—Created Debit column and is deducted from amount in the Balance Credit column. Subsequently, as the order is received and the amount of the actual expenditure is determined, the encumbrance is cancelled by entering the amount of the encumbrance in the Encumbrance—Liquidated Credit column. At the same time, the actual expenditure is recorded by entering the amount of the expenditure in the Expenditures Debit column. The Encumbrances—Liquidated Credit entry and the Expenditures Debit entry are simultaneously added to and deducted from the amount in the Balance Credit column.

TYPICAL ACCOUNT BALANCES

Figure 8 is a summary of the types of accounts discussed in this text with their normal balances and how they are increased and decreased indicated by the T-accounts above the accounts.

EXAMPLE OF A REVENUES SUBSIDIARY LEDGER

The following example illustrates the use of the Revenues Subsidiary Ledger.

CITY OF METROPOLIS
GENERAL FUND

A. The Council estimated that revenue of $200,000 would be gathered for the General Fund in 19X5. The sources and amounts of expected revenue are as follows:

Property tax revenue	$148,500
Parking meter revenue	6,000
Liquor licenses	22,500
Motor vehicle licenses	23,000
	$200,000

B. The Council levied property taxes of $150,000 but expected that $1,500 would prove uncollectible.

C. The City made the following collections:

Property taxes revenue	$128,500
Parking meter revenue	7,000
Liquor licenses	21,000
Motor vehicle licenses	24,500
	$181,000

Requirements

1. Record the transactions in the General Journal.
2. Post to the General Ledger accounts, Estimated Revenue and Revenue.
3. Post to the Revenues Subsidiary Ledger. (Use three-column accounts.)
4. Prepare a list of the balances in the Revenues Subsidiary Ledger after the postings. (Show agreement with the control accounts.)
5. Make the closing entry for the revenue accounts; it is not necessary to close the accounts in the subsidiary ledger.

CITY OF METROPOLIS
GENERAL FUND
GENERAL JOURNAL

page 1

A.	Estimated Revenues		200,000.00	
	Fund Balance			200,000.00
	To record the estimated revenues			
	portion of the budget.			

Debit Revenues
  Subsidiary Ledger:

Property Tax Revenues	148,500
Parking Meter Revenues	6,000
Liquor Licenses	22,500
Motor Vehicle Licenses	23,000
	200,000

B.	Taxes Receivable—Current		150,000.00	
	Estimated Uncollectible			
	Taxes—Current			1,500.00
	Revenues			148,500.00
	To record levy of property taxes.			

Credit Revenues
  Subsidiary Ledger:

Property Tax Revenues	148,500

C.	Cash		181,000.00	
	Taxes Receivable—Current			128,500.00
	Revenues			52,500.00
	To record collections of revenues.			

Credit Revenues
  Subsidiary Ledger:

Parking Meter Revenues	7,000
Liquor Licenses	21,000
Motor Vehicle Licenses	24,500
	52,500

Cl.	Revenues		201,000.00	
	Estimated Revenues			200,000.00
	Fund Balance			1,000.00
	To close revenues into fund balance.			

CITY OF METROPOLIS
GENERAL FUND
GENERAL LEDGER

Cash

Tr.	C	1	181,000.00

Taxes Receivable—Current

Tr.	B	1	150,000.00	Tr.	C	1	128,500.00

Estimated Uncollectible Taxes

		Tr.	B	1	1,500.00

Fund Balance

		Tr.	A	1	200,000.00
		Tr.	Cl.	1	1,000.00

Estimated Revenues

Tr.	A	1	200,000.00	Tr.	Cl.	1	200,000.00

Revenues

Tr.	Cl.	1	201,000.00	Tr.	B	1	148,500.00
				Tr.	C	1	52,500.00
			201,000.00				201,000.00

CITY OF METROPOLIS
GENERAL FUND
REVENUES SUBSIDIARY LEDGER

Property Tax Revenues

Date	Description	Post Ref.	Estimated Debit	Actual Credit	Balance Debit
Tr. A		GJ1	148,500.00		148,500.00
Tr. B		GJ1		148,500.00	—0—

Parking Meter Revenues

Date	Description	Post Ref.	Estimated Debit	Actual Credit	Balance Debit
Tr. A		GJ1	6,000.00		6,000.00
Tr. C		GJ1		7,000.00	<1,000.00>

Liquor Licenses

Date	Description	Post Ref.	Estimated Debit	Actual Credit	Balance Debit
Tr. A		GJ1	22,500.00		22,500.00
Tr. C		GJ1		21,000.00	1,500.00

Motor Vehicle Licenses

Date	Description	Post Ref.	Estimated Debit	Actual Credit	Balance Debit
Tr. A		GJ1	23,000.00		23,000.00
Tr. C		GJ1		24,500.00	<1,500.00>

CITY OF METROPOLIS
GENERAL FUND
REVENUES SUBSIDIARY LEDGER
ACCOUNT BALANCES
December 31, 19X5

	Debit <Credit> Balance
Property Tax Revenues	— 0 —
Parking Meter Revenues	<1,000.00>
Liquor Licenses	1,500.00
Motor Vehicle Licenses	<1,500.00>
Balance	<1,000.00>

CITY OF METROPOLIS
GENERAL FUND
BALANCES OF CONTROL ACCOUNTS
FOR REVENUES SUBSIDIARY LEDGER
GENERAL LEDGER
December 31, 19X5

	Debit *<Credit>* *Balance*
Estimated Revenues	200,000.00
Revenues	<201,000.00>
Balance	<1,000.00>

EXAMPLE OF AN EXPENDITURES SUBSIDIARY LEDGER

The following example illustrates the use of an Expenditures Subsidiary Ledger.

CITY OF NOLAND
GENERAL FUND

A.   The Council made appropriations of $197,000 for the year 19X7 as follows:

Council		
Personal Services	18,000	
Contractual Services	3,000	
Materials and Supplies	9,000	
Other Charges	12,000	42,000
Executive Department		
Personal Services	27,000	
Contractual Services	34,000	
Materials and Supplies	17,000	
Other Charges	12,000	90,000
Interest on Debt		15,000
Retirement of Debt		50,000
		197,000

B.   Purchase orders were placed as follows:

Council		
Materials and Supplies	6,000	
Executive Department		
Contractual Services	20,000	
Materials and Supplies	10,000	36,000

C.   Actual expenditures, including all of the purchase orders except $2,500 of Materials and Supplies for the Executive Department, were as follows:

Council		
Personal Services	17,700	
Contractual Services	3,000	
Materials and Supplies	8,800	
Other Charges	11,900	41,400
Executive Department		
Personal Services	27,000	
Contractual Services	33,800	
Materials and Supplies	13,900	
Other Charges	11,900	86,600
Interest on Debt		15,000
Retirement of Debt		50,000
		193,000

Requirements

1.   Record the transactions for the year in the General Journal.
2.   Post to the control accounts and to the Appropriations–Expenditures Subsidiary Ledger.
3.   Take a trial balance of the accounts in the Appropriations–Expenditures Subsidiary Ledger as of the last day of the year. Balance it with the control accounts.
4.   Close out the Appropriations and Appropriation Expenditures accounts.

CITY OF NOLAND
GENERAL FUND
GENERAL JOURNAL

A.	Fund Balance	197,000.00	
	Appropriations		197,000.00
	To record the appropriations		
	for the budget.		

Credit Appropriations—Expenditures
  Subsidiary Ledger:

Council—Personal Services	18,000
Council—Contractual Services	3,000
Council—Materials and Supplies	9,000
Council—Other Charges	12,000
Exec. Dept.—Personal Services	27,000
Exec. Dept.—Contractual Services	34,000
Exec. Dept.—Materials and Supplies	17,000
Exec. Dept.—Other Charges	12,000
Interest on Debt	15,000
Retirement of Debt	50,000
	197,000

B.	Encumbrances	36,000.00	
	Reserve for Encumbrances		36,000.00
	To record encumbrance.		

Debit Appropriations—Expenditures
  Subsidiary Ledger:

Council—Materials and Supplies	6,000
Exec. Dept.—Contractual Services	20,000
Exec. Dept.—Materials and Supplies	10,000
	36,000

C. Reserve for Encumbrances   33,500.00
        Encumbrances   33,500.00
    To record cancellation of encumbrances.

    Credit Appropriations—Expenditures
      Subsidiary Ledger:
        Council—Materials and Supplies   6,000
        Exec. Dept.—Contractual
          Services   20,000
        Exec. Dept.—Materials and
          Supplies   7,500
                                           ——————
                                           33,500
                                           ══════

    Expenditures   193,000.00
        Vouchers Payable   193,000.00
    To record preparation of voucher.

    Debit Appropriations—Expenditures
      Subsidiary Ledger:
        Council—Personal Services   17,700
        Council—Contractual Services   3,000
        Council—Materials and Supplies   8,800
        Council—Other Charges   11,900
        Exec. Dept.—Personal Services   27,000
        Exec. Dept.—Contractual
          Services   33,800
        Exec. Dept.—Materials and
          Supplies   13,900
        Exec. Dept.—Other Charges   11,900
        Interest on Debt   15,000
        Retirement of Debt   50,000
                                          ——————
                                          193,000
                                          ══════

CI. Appropriations   197,000.00
        Expenditures   193,000.00
        Encumbrances   2,500.00
        Fund Balance   1,500.00
    To record closing of appropriations,
    expenditures, and encumbrances into
    fund balance.

CITY OF NOLAND
GENERAL FUND
GENERAL LEDGER

Appropriations

Tr.	Cl.	2	197,000.00	Tr.	A	1	197,000.00

Expenditures

Tr.	C	2	193,000.00	Tr.	C(Cl)	2	193,000.00

Encumbrances

Tr.	B	1	36,000.00	Tr.	C	2	33,500.00
				Tr.	C(Cl)	2	2,500.00
			36,000.00				36,000.00

CITY OF NOLAND
GENERAL FUND
APPROPRIATIONS—EXPENDITURES SUBSIDIARY LEDGER

Date	Description	Encumbrances		Expenditures	Appropriations	Balance
		Created Debit	Liquidated Credit	Debit	Credit	Credit
Council—Personal Services						
Tr. A					18,000.00	18,000.00
Tr. C				17,700.00		300.00
Council—Contractual Services						
Tr. A					3,000.00	3,000.00
Tr. C				3,000.00		—0—
Council—Materials and Supplies						
Tr. A					9,000.00	9,000.00
Tr. B		6,000.00				3,000.00
Tr. C			6,000.00			9,000.00
Tr. C				8,800.00		200.00

Date	Description	Encumbrances		Expenditures Debt	Appropriations Credit	Balance Credit
		Created Debit	Liquidated Credit			
Council—Other Charges						
Tr. A					12,000.00	12,000.00
Tr. C				11,900.00		100.00
Executive Department—Personal Services						
Tr. A					27,000.00	27,000.00
Tr. C				27,000.00		—0—
Executive Department—Contractual Services						
Tr. A					34,000.00	34,000.00
Tr. B		20,000.00				14,000.00
Tr. C			20,000.00			34,000.00
Tr. C				33,800.00		200.00
Executive Department—Materials and Supplies						
Tr. A					17,000.00	17,000.00
Tr. B		10,000.00				7,000.00
Tr. C			7,500.00			14,500.00
Tr. C				13,900.00		600.00
Executive Department—Other Charges						
Tr. A					12,000.00	12,000.00
Tr. C				11,900.00		100.00
Interest on Debt						
Tr. A					15,000.00	15,000.00
Tr. C				15,000.00		—0—
Retirement of Debt						
Tr. A					50,000.00	50,000.00
Tr. C				50,000.00		—0—

GENERAL FUND
APPROPRIATIONS—EXPENDITURES SUBSIDIARY LEDGER
ACCOUNT BALANCES
December 31, 19X7

	Debit <Credit> Balance
Council—Personal Services	300.00
Council—Contractual Services	-0-
Council—Materials and Supplies	200.00
Council—Other·Charges	100.00
Executive Department—Personal Services	-0-
Executive Department—Contractual Services	200.00
Executive Department—Materials and Supplies	600.00
Executive Department—Other Charges	100.00
Interest on Debt	-0-
Retirement of Debt	-0-
Balance	1,500.00

GENERAL FUND
BALANCES OF CONTROL ACCOUNTS
FOR APPROPRIATIONS—EXPENDITURES SUBSIDIARY LEDGER
GENERAL LEDGER
December 31, 19X7

		Credit <Debit> Balance
Appropriations		197,000.00
Expenditures	193,000.00	
Encumbrances	2,500.00	<195,500.00>
Balance		1,500.00

Problem 9-1

Expenditures
Subsidiary Ledger Account

An appropriation was made by the Council for supplies for $9,000.
During the year 19X5 these transactions occurred:

1. The Council ordered $4,000 (estimated cost) of supplies on January 10, 19X5, with Order Number 72.

2. The Council ordered $2,000 (estimated cost) of supplies on January 29, 19X5, with Order Number 73.

3. On February 12, 19X5, Order Number 72 arrived. Its actual cost was $4,300.

4. On March 2, 19X5, Order Number 73 arrived. Its actual cost was $1,900.

5. On October 5, 19X5, the Council bought some supplies for cash. Cost was $2,600.

6. The City receives a $100 quantity discount for the supplies bought for the Council.

Requirements

Prepare an Expenditures Subsidiary Ledger account for Council's supplies.

Problem 9-2

City AAA
Use of a Subsidiary Ledger
Estimated Revenues—Actual Revenues

1. The Council estimated that revenue of $150,000 would be generated for the General Fund in 19X7. Appropriations for the year were $145,000. The sources and amounts of expected revenue are as follows:

Property Tax Revenue	$ 90,000
Parking Meter Revenue	5,000
Business Licenses	30,000
Amusement Licenses	10,000
Beer Licenses	15,000
	$150,000

2. Property taxes of $91,000 were levied by the Council. $1,000 of property taxes are expected to be uncollectible.

3. The following collections were made by the City:

Property taxes	$ 80,000
Parking meters	5,500
Business licenses	28,000
Amusement licenses	9,500
Beer license	18,000
	$141,000

Requirements

1. Record the transactions in the General Journal.
2. Post to the General Ledger control accounts.
3. Post to the Revenues Subsidiary Ledger.
4. Prepare a trial balance of the balances in the Revenues Subsidiary Ledger after the postings. (Show agreement with the control accounts.)
5. Make the closing entry for the revenue accounts in the General Journal.

Problem 9-3

CITY OF LYNN
GENERAL FUND

The General Fund of the City of Lynn had the following account balances on December 31, 19X9:

Cash	$ 1,000
Fund Balance	1,000

1. On January 1, 19X0, the City Council approved the following budget:

Revenues:	
Property Taxes	$50,000
Miscellaneous	2,500
	$52,500
Expenditures:	
Mayor's Office	$14,000
Police Department	28,000
Sanitation Department	10,000
	$52,000

2. Taxes were levied in the amount of $50,000. It was estimated that 4 percent of this amount would prove uncollectible.
3. Orders were placed as follows:

Mayor's Office	$12,000
Police Department	27,500
Sanitation Department	8,000
	$47,500

4. Invoices vouchered during the year are listed as follows:

Mayor's Office	$12,500
Police Department	29,000
Sanitation Department	8,000
Refund on Overassessment of Taxes	500
	$50,000

5. Collections during the year were from the following sources:

Taxes Levied during 19X0	$49,000
Interest and Penalties on Taxes	900
Service Charges	2,200
Refund on Defective Police Equipment Returned	500
	$52,600

The foregoing invoices complete all orders placed during 19X0 with the exception of a $300 item ordered by the Police Department.

6. Analysis of collections revealed that Taxpayer A, to whom the city had refunded $500 for the overpayment of taxes, had not been properly assessed and actually owed the city an additional $500. A total of $1,000 must now be assessed.

Requirements

1. Prepare journal entries to record the foregoing transactions.
2. Post to T-accounts.
3. Post to the appropriate subsidiary ledger accounts.
4. Reconcile the subsidiary accounts with their respective control accounts.
5. Prepare a preclosing trial balance.

Problem 9-4

CITY OF JACKSON
GENERAL FUND

The following information summarizes the operations of the General Fund of the City of Jackson for the year ended December 31, 19X7:

1. The account balances at December 31, 19X6, were as follows:

Cash	$ 5,000
Reserve for Encumbrances	1,500
Fund Balance	3,500

2. The City Council estimated the following revenues for 19X7:

Property Taxes	$100,000
Licenses	25,000
Fines and Fees	10,000
	$135,000

3. Planned expenditures for 19X7 were as follows:

General Administration	$ 80,000
Police Department	20,000
Streets and Roads	25,000
	$125,000

4. Taxes in the amount of $110,000 were levied. It was expected that $5,000 of these taxes would prove uncollectible.

5. Receipts during the year consisted of the following:

Property Taxes	$103,000
Licenses	25,000
Fines and Fees	8,000
	$136,000

6. The following purchase orders were placed:

General Administration	$ 50,000
Police Department	20,000
Streets and Roads	15,000
	$ 85,000

7. A snow plow blade ordered in the preceding year was received. It was invoiced to the City at $1,500.

8. The following orders were received:

	Originally Ordered	Vouchered
General Administration	$ 45,000	$ 44,000
Police Department	20,000	20,000
Streets and Roads	15,000	15,500
	$ 80,000	$ 79,500

9. Additional vouchers were prepared for the following purposes:

General Administration	$ 30,000
Streets and Roads	9,000
	$ 39,000

10. Vouchers were paid in the total amount of $113,000.

Requirements

1. Record transactions in the General Journal.
2. Post to the General Ledger, Revenues Subsidiary Ledger, and Expenditures Subsidiary Ledger.
3. Prepare a trial balance of the General Ledger.
4. Reconcile the subsidiary ledgers with their control accounts.
5. Prepare closing entries.
6. Post to the ledgers.
7. Prepare a balance sheet after closing.
8. Prepare a statement of revenues—estimated and actual. (See standard text.)
9. Prepare a statement of expenditures and encumbrances compared with appropriations. (See standard text.)
10. Prepare an analysis of changes in fund balance.

Problem 9-5

CITY OF AHL
GENERAL FUND

The account balances of the City of Ahl at December 31, 19X6, were as follows:

Cash	$ 2,000
Reserve for Encumbrances	800
Fund Balance	1,200

The following transactions took place in the City of Ahl during 19X7:

1. The Council estimated that revenue of $100,000 would be generated for the General
    Fund. The sources and amounts of expected revenue were as follows:

Property Tax Revenue	$ 75,000
Fines	10,000
Amusement Licenses	15,000
	$100,000

    The Council made appropriations of $98,000 as follows:

General Administration	$ 70,000
Recreation Department	20,000
Street Department	8,000
	$ 89,000

2. The Council levied property taxes of $76,000 but estimated that $1,000 would prove
    uncollectible.

3. The following purchase orders were placed:

General Administration	$ 50,000
Recreation Department	15,000
Street Department	4,000
	$ 69,000

4. The following amounts were received during the year:

Property Taxes	$ 76,000
Fines	10,000
Amusement Licenses	16,000
	$102,000

5. The order placed for the Street Department in 19X6 was received; the invoice indicated
    an actual cost of $900.

6. The following 19X7 orders were received:

	Encumbrances Liquidated	Expenditures
General Administration	$45,000	$46,000
Recreation Department	15,000	15,000
Street Department	3,500	3,700
	$63,500	$64,700

7. Additional vouchers were prepared for the following purposes:

General Administration	$ 20,000
Recreation Department	2,000
Street Department	5,500
Refund on Overpayment of Taxes	800
	$ 28,300

8. Vouchers were paid in the total amount of $93,000.

Requirements

1. **Prepare the General Journal.**
2. **Post to ledger accounts. (Use three columns for the Revenues Subsidiary Ledger and five columns for the Appropriations–Expenditures Subsidiary Ledger.)**
3. **Prepare the preclosing trial balance.**
4. **Reconcile subsidiary ledgers with control accounts.**
5. **Journalize closing entries.**
6. **Prepare, after closing on December 31, 19X7,**
   a. **Postclosing trial balance.**
   b. **Analysis of changes in fund balance.**
   c. **Statement of revenues—estimated and actual.**
   d. **Statement of expenditures and encumbrances compared with appropriations.**
   e. **Balance sheet.**

Problem 9-6

CITY OF TREJO

The following is a trial balance of the General Fund of the City of Trejo as of December 31, 19X9 after closing entries:

Cash	$31,000	
Taxes Receivable—Delinquent	12,000	
Estimated Uncollectible Taxes—		
Delinquent		$ 8,500
Interest and Penalties Receivable	550	
Estimated Uncollectible Interest		
and Penalties		475
Vouchers Payable		8,000
Due to Stores Fund		150
Fund Balance		23,600
Reserve for Encumbrances		2,825
	$43,550	$43,550

The following transactions took place during 19X0:

1. Revenues were estimated at $753,000; appropriations were set at $750,000. The Council estimated that revenue of $753,000 would be generated for the General Fund. The sources and amounts of expected revenues were as follows:

Property Taxes	$743,000
License Permits	3,000
Miscellaneous	7,000

The Council made appropriations of $750,000 as follows:

Mayor's Office	$275,000
Police Department	200,000
Fire Department	125,000
Sanitation Department	100,000
Parks and Recreation Department	50,000

2. Taxes amounting to $760,000 were levied. An allowance of 2 percent was made for estimated losses.
3. A correction is necessary due to an overassessment that was made in the amount of $1,000; the taxpayer had not yet sent in the payment.
4. Serial bonds amounting to $10,000 matured; charge to Mayor's Office in the subsidiary ledger.
5. An order for two garbage trucks was placed; the estimated cost was $35,000.
6. An order placed in the preceding year was received; the invoice amount is $2,900.
7. A note was signed at the bank in the amount of $20,000.
8. Collections were made:

Current taxes	$710,000
Delinquent taxes	5,000
Interest and penalties	125
License permits	2,000
Traffic citations	3,850
Miscellaneous	425

9. An order was placed to have the Mayor's Offices air conditioned; the cost is estimated at $20,000. Two police cars were ordered at an estimated cost of $10,500.

10. The note at the bank was paid in full.

11. It was discovered that a taxpayer had been overassessed $500; he had already sent in the payment. Prepare a voucher to correct this error.

12. Payments were made as follows:

Salaries	$515,000
Garbage Trucks	36,500
Vouchers Payable	2,900

Salaries were prorated as follows:

Mayor's Office	$200,000
Police Department	150,000
Fire Department	100,000
Sanitation Department	30,000
Parks and Recreation Department	35,000

13. Collection of delinquent taxes of $1,800 plus interest and penalties of $115, all of which had been previously written off as uncollectible was made; credit to miscellaneous account in the subsidiary ledger.

14. Taxes receivable (current) have been designated as uncollectable in the amount of $10,000

15. A taxpayer was reimbursed in the amount of $100 for an overpayment; no error was made on the part of the City.

16. All taxes not collected at this time should be changed to delinquent status.

17. Matured serial bonds were paid.

18. Received supplies for Parks and Recreation Department from Stores in the amount of $110.

19. Payments were made as follows:

Interest (Mayor's Office)	$ 2,000
Balance due Stores Fund	(to be determined)
Salaries	$145,000

Salaries were prorated as follows:

Mayor's Office	$ 45,000
Police Department	35,000
Fire Department	15,000
Sanitation Department	35,000
Parks and Recreation Department	15,000

20. Delinquent taxes of $10,000 were written off as uncollectible.
21. Pay all outstanding vouchers.
22. Placed an order for miscellaneous equipment for the Fire Department in the amount of $8,000.

Requirements

1. Record the opening trial balance in the amounts.
2. Prepare journal entries for the transactions.
3. Post to accounts.
4. Prepare a trial balance.
5. Reconcile subsidiary ledgers with control accounts.
6. Prepare closing entries.
7. Post closing entries to the accounts.
8. Prepare a postclosing trial balance.
9. Prepare a balance sheet.
10. Prepare an analysis of changes in fund balance statement.

INDEX

A

Account
    balances, determining,   12
    chart of normal balances,   6, 105-106
    described,   5
    illustrated,   11
Accounting
    cycle,   27
    defined,   1
    equation,   2-3, 24
Accounting, governmental; see Fund accounting
Analysis of Changes in Fund Balance, illustrated,   92, 94-95, 96
Appropriations
    lapsing-nonlapsing,   56-57, 62
    recording of,   45
Assets, defined,   2